D1860138

INDIA NIGERIA TRADE RELATIONS (2000-2013)

India Nigeria Trade Relations (2000-2013)

Sanju Prasad

GenNext Publication

© **Author**
All rights reserved. No part of this book may be reproduced, stored, adapted, or transmitted in any form or by any means, electronic, mechanical, photocopying, micro-filming recording or otherwise, or translated in any language, without the prior written permission of the copyright owner and the publisher. The book is sold subject to the condition that it shall not, by way of trade or otherwise, be lent, resold, hired out, or otherwise circulated without the prior publisher's written consent in any form of binding or cover other than that in which it is published.

The views and opinions expressed in this book are author(s) own and the facts reported by them have been verified to the extent possible, and the publishers are not in any way liable for the same.

ISBN : 978-93-8022-254-7

Price : ₹ 580

First Published in 2015

Published by

GenNext Publication
23, Main Ansari Road, Darya Ganj
New Delhi-110002
Ph. : 23282060, 23261060
Fax : 011-23285914
E-mail: gennext@hotmail.com

Laser Typesetting : Abhishek Mondal, Delhi
Printed at : Sagar Color Scan, Delhi

Cataloging in Publication Data—DK

Courtesy: D.K. Agencies (P) Ltd. <docinfo@dkagencies.com>

Prasad, Sanju, author.

India Nigeria trade relations (2000-2013) / Sanju Prasad.

pages cm

Includes bibliographical references (pages) and index.

ISBN 9789380222547

1. India—Commerce—Nigeria—History—21st century. 2. Nigeria—Commerce—India—History—21st century. I. Title.

DDC 382.09540669 23

Contents

List of Tables

List of Charts and Figures

Acronyms

AIIMS	-	All India Institute of Medical Sciences
API	-	Australian Pharmaceutical Industries
ARV	-	Anti Retroviral
ATC	-	Automation, Telecommunication and Computing
AU	-	Africa Union
AUC	-	Administrative Uniformity Committee
AWA	-	AIDS Watch Africa
BCA	-	Bachelor in Computer Applications
BMI	-	Business Monitor Internationals
BPAP	-	Business Process Association of the Philippines
BPRL	-	Bharat Petroleum Corporation Limited
CCM	-	Country Co-ordinating Mechanism
CDM	-	Clean Development Mechanism

CIDA	-	Canadian International Development Agency
CII	-	Confederation of Indian Industry
CIS	-	Commonwealth of Independent States
CME	-	Continuing Medical Education
CNOOC	-	China National Offshore Oil Corporation
CSIR	-	Council of Scientific and Industrial Research
DFID	-	Department for International Development
DHA	-	Development Assistance to Health
EAM	-	Enterprise Asset Management
ECCDE	-	Early Childhood Care and Development
ECOWAS	-	Economic of West African States
EIA	-	Energy Information Administration
ESC	-	Educational Service Center
ETF	-	Exchange Traded Fund
FCT	-	Federal Capital Territory
FDI	-	Foreign Direct Investment
FICCI	-	Federation of Indian Chambers of Commerce and Industry
GAIL	-	Gas Authority of India Limited
GASSCOM	-	Ghana Association of Software and IT Services Companies
GDP	-	Gross Domestic Product

GGHE/GGE	-	General Government Health Expenditure/General Government Expenditure
GNIIT	-	Graduate from National Institute of Information Technology
GoI	-	Government of India
HC	-	High Commission
HIV/AIDS	-	Human Immunodeficiency Virus Infection/Acquired Immune Deficiency Syndrome
HPCL	-	Hindustan Petroleum Corporation Limited
IAFS	-	India-Africa Forum Summit
ICC	-	Indigenous Cultural Competency
ICT	-	Information and Communication Technology
IDC	-	International Data Corporation
IMNCH	-	Integrated Maternal Newborn and Child Health
IOCL	-	Indian Oil Corporation Limited
IS	-	Information Services
IT	-	Information Technology
ITAN	-	Information Technology Association of Nigeria
IT-BPO	-	Information Technology and Business Process Outsourcing Sector
ITEC	-	Indian Technical and Economic Co-operation Programme

ITES	-	Information Technology and Enabled Services
JCI	-	Joint Commission International
KAM	-	Knowledge Assessment Methodology
KE	-	Knowledge Economy
LASIK	-	Laser-Assisted in Situ Keratomileusis
LGA	-	Local Government Areas
LNG	-	Liquefied Natural Gas
LOCs	-	Lines of Credit
M.Sc	-	Master of Science
MBA	-	Master of Business Administration
MCA	-	Master in Computer Applications
MCC	-	Medicines Control Council
MDAs	-	Media Development Authority
MDG	-	Million Development Goal Target
MEA	-	Ministry of External Affairs
MIS	-	Management Information Services
MMSCMD	-	Million Metric Standard Cubic Meter Per Day
MOS	-	Ministry of State
MOU	-	Memorandum of Understanding
NEPAD	-	New Economic Partnership for Africa's Development
NESAP-ICT	-	New Economy Skills for Africa Programme: Information and Communication Technology

NEXIMB	-	Nigerian Export Import Bank
NIIT	-	National Institute of Information Technology
NITDA	-	National Information Technology Development Agency
NOC	-	National Oil Corporation
NTPC	-	National Thermal Power Corporation
ODIN	-	Outsourcing Development Initiative of Nigeria
OIFC	-	Overseas Indian Facilitation Center
OMEL	-	ONGC Mittal Energy Limited
ONGC	-	Oil and Natural Gas Corporation
OPEC	-	Organisation of the Petroleum Exporting Countries
ONGCVL	-	ONGC Videsh Limited
PAENP	-	Pan African e-Network Project
PG	-	Post Graduate
PHARM EXCIL	-	Pharmaceuticals Export Promotion Council of India
PHC	-	Primary Health Care
PIB	-	Press Information Bureau
PSU	-	Power Supply Unit
R and D	-	Research and Development
RA	-	Rheumatoid Arthritis
RECS	-	Renewable Energy Certificate System
S and T	-	Science and Technology

SCAAP	-	Special Commonwealth Assistance for Africa Programme
SME	-	Medium Enterprises
SSC	-	South-South Co-operation
TB	-	Tuberculosis
TCIL	-	Telecommunications Consultants India Ltd.
UG	-	Under Graduate
UK	-	United Kingdom
UNAIDS	-	United Nations Programme on HIV/AIDS
UNDP	-	United Nations Development Programme
UNFPA	-	United Nations Populations Fund
USA	-	United States of America
USFDA	-	US Food and Drug Administration
WHO	-	World Health Organisation
WTO	-	World Trade Organisation

Acknowledgements

I acknowledge with gratitude the efforts of my supervisor, Dr Renu Modi who always helped and supported me throughout my dissertation work. She was always encouraging and enabled the timely submission of my dissertation. My guide has always taught me to respect deadlines and move ahead for better opportunities. I thank her once again for reposing her trust in me and being with me when I needed her the most. She always took time out of her work schedule and gave priority to working with me on my dissertation so that I could research on the subject and complete this dissertation within the stipulated timeframe.

Sincere thanks also go to my friends and fellow M. Phil students; Sarita Kadam, Vinita Hede, Chandni Shiyal and Anjali Kapse, for helping me during the completion process of my book.

My entire family has been of great help throughout my studies. Special thanks go to my parents Doodhnath Prasad and Ramavati Prasad for their moral and financial support.

I thank Sarita Yadav, Kavita Sharma, Chitra Gadgil, Ashish Upadhyay, Vandana Ude, Sarita Maurya, Tarannum Shaikh, Swapna Singh, Vibha Singh, Pranita Jadhav and Priyanka Khartmal who always said, "You can do it", and their support have been a great source of inspiration for me. I also thank Prachi Chavan (Documentation Assistant, Centre for African Studies, University of Mumbai) for helping me with the technical part of my book.

Preface

Since I completed my Masters in Sociology, I enrolled in African Studies for M.Phil. course with curiosity and trepidation about Africa. As I finished my course work I got acquainted with the countries on the continent of Africa and the upward trend in the trade relations between India-Africa, in particular between India-Nigeria. Besides, both the countries are emerging economies with a positive forecast with regard to economic growth. A notable aspect of India-Nigeria is the reciprocal nature of their bilateral and symbiotic relationship between the two partners. India and Nigeria co-operate in several sectors inter-alia; power, industry, agriculture, energy, Information and Communication Technology (ICT) and health. Further, about 20 Indian ICT sector firms have invested in excess of N̈3 trillion within the last eight years (2005-2012).

I also noted that over the past decades the West African state of Nigeria has been one of the steady and major sources of energy security for India. India is Nigeria's second largest trading partner and Nigeria has also remained India's largest trading partner in Africa. It has improved its position to of the rank as the 13th largest global trading partner of India.

The volume of trade between the two countries stood at $19.5 billion in 2013 and there has been an increase in the volume of trade and bilateral relations have deepened with Nigeria in spite of the security challenges within the country. The volume of trade between the two partners is expected to rise to $20 billion before the end of 2014.

Nigeria is the second largest supplier of oil to India, after the Middle East region. New initiatives, such as India-Africa Forum Summits of 2008 and 2011 between India and African countries are efforts towards further entrenching their old relationship. For oil producing countries like Nigeria, where the economy is heavily dependent on the hydrocarbon sector, new initiatives outlined in Nigeria's vision document 20:2020, aims to grow Nigeria's market share in the world economy and in this strategy India is a favoured destination for the exports of crude hydrocarbons.

In the health segment, major hospitals such as the Primus in Abuja and other diagnostic clinics run by Indian doctors provide healthcare to the Nigerian populace. Many Nigerians also seek treatment in India and come as 'medical tourists'. Besides, India's pharmaceuticals and medicare industry is contributing towards building capacity in Nigeria. The research findings of my M.Phil thesis culminated in the form of this book. This research work are a humble contribution towards highlighting the emerging India-Nigeria relations. Where in both the countries complement each other's development trajectory that is mutually beneficial to the people of the two countries under study.

1

Introduction

Nigeria is one of the major oil exporters in Africa, with the largest natural gas reserves on the continent. With these large reserves of human and natural resources, Nigeria is poised to build a prosperous economy, significantly reduce poverty, and provide health, education and infrastructure services to its population needs (The World Bank, 2013a). Nigeria is the most populous country in Africa with a population of more than 168.8 million (The World Bank, 2013b). It is the largest country in Africa and accounts for 47 per cent of West Africa's population. A common theme in most investment discussions involving Nigeria is demographic. The large population of the country makes Nigeria a potential market for fast moving consumer goods, basic financial services and infrastructure investments that the country needs.

Nigeria is India's one of the largest trading partner in Africa. This book studies trade relations between the two partners for over the past decade i.e., 2000-2013. It deals with three sectors in India and Nigeria relations, namely; energy, health, and capacity building in the Information and Communications Technology (ICT) education. It examines the politico-diplomatic, socio-cultural and economic relations between India and Nigeria and a looks into their enhanced engagement that will heighten and redefine economic relations between the two countries. The underlying argument of this research is that economic cooperation would not only strengthen their political relations but also bring mutual benefits to both the countries.

India had established its diplomatic representation with Nigeria in 1958 even before Nigeria attained independence in 1960. The establishment of diplomatic relations two years prior to Nigeria's independence, laid the foundation for what led, friendly and concrete bilateral relations between India and Nigeria. The diplomatic and commercial visits between officials of the two countries crystallised and concretised their co-operative ties centered around political around political, economic and socio-cultural issues (MEA 2014: p.1).

Diplomatic Relations: Since the early 20th century there have been visible demonstrations of friendship between the two countries. During October 2010, the Indian High Commission in Nigeria estimated that 35,000 Indians were living in Nigeria. There are also many Nigerians living in India. Diplomatic friendship is evident in numerous exchanges and visits between leaders of both sides and the important new phase has occurred in diplomatic links between Nigeria and India. Visits of Nigerian officials to India have been to gain knowledge and understanding about India's infra-structural development, science and technology, poverty eradication measures and labour issues. Nigeria also solicited support from India for the appointment of the Nigerian finance minister, Dr. Ngozi Okonjo-Iweala candidature for the President of the World Bank. In April 2008, 'President Goodluck EbeleAzikiwe Jonathan visited India to attend the India-Africa Forum Summit' (Alao: SAIIA 2011: pp. 12-13).

Political dignitaries such as the former President Olusegun Obasanjo had paid a state visit to India in January 2000 and a working visit in November 2004. To promote good relations, India's current Prime Minister Dr. Manmohan Singh paid a reciprocal state visit in October 2007 to Nigeria that gave a new fillip to the bilateral ties. During this visit the Nigeria and India Joint Commission was resurrected and the Abuja Declaration on Strategic Partnership was signed (Kura 2009: 10; see also MEA 2014). This led to a new phase in diplomatic links between Nigeria and India (Alao: SAIIA 2011: pp. 12-13).

These high level political visits are of significance and indicate the earnest desire on the part of both the partners to promote and keep alive their good political and economic relations. There is an active Nigeria and India Joint Commission that meets every two years. In January 2010, Minister for Commerce and Industry Shri Anand Sharma and Minister for Petroleum and Natural Gas Shri Murli Deora travelled to Nigeria to attend the 'Namaskar Africa' event (Vines et. al 2009: p.10; see also SAIIA 2011: pp.12-13). A high level visit by India's Petroleum Minister shows the importance India attaches to Nigeria as a source of energy security that is so essential for India's economy.

Commercial and Trade Relations: India is currently Nigeria's second largest trading partner. Nigeria is also the largest market in Africa for Indian exports. A host of Indian companies are engaged there and they have sizeable investments in textiles, chemicals, electrical equipments etc. These Indian companies are: Bharti Airtel, Indorama, Olam International, Tata Group, Bajaj Auto, Birla Group, Mahindra, Pharmaceutical companies, NIIT, APTECH, New India Assurance, Bhushan Steel, KEC International Ltd., Skipper Nigeria, Dabur, Godrej and Primus

Super-Speciality Hospitals (MEA 2014: p. 3). In addition the annual trade turnover between the two partners was over $ 17.3 billion in 2011-12 and registered a growth of over 34 per cent. During 2012-13, Indian exports grew by 1.33 per cent even though the bilateral trades declined slightly to $ 16.8 billion (Vines *et.al* 2009: p. 10; see also MEA 2014: p. 2).

***Economic Community of West African States (ECOWAS)*:** Nigeria's emerging economic relations revolve around its role in supplying other economies with oil and natural gas, even as the country seeks to diversify its exports, harmonise tariffs in line with a potential customs union sought by the ECOWAS and encourage inflows of foreign portfolio and direct investment. Over the past decade, the makeup of Nigeria's donors and investors has changed significantly, with new entrants from countries of the South are playing an increasingly important role. China, India, Brazil and other developing countries are providing Nigeria with new sources of financing, enabling Nigeria to lessen its dependence on traditional donors from countries of the North (Afribiz Media, 2012).

With growing relationship between India and Nigeria, several sectors are opening up for further cooperation between the two. The major economic sectors of Nigeria include:

1. Crude petroleum and natural gas;
2. Telecommunication and post;
3. Manufacturing;
4. Finance and business services;
5. Health sector; and
6. Wholesale and retail trade (Focus Africa 2010).

Though, all of the above sectors are important for India and Nigeria economic relations, the focus of this book will be on three major areas of economic cooperation namely; the energy, health and the education sectors.

A Focus on Energy Security: Nigeria plays an important role in Indian economy due to its crude oil exports to India. India is currently Nigeria's second largest trading partner and Nigeria earns considerable revenues from oil exports (MEA 2012b: p.1). India is one of the key players in Africa. India maintains relationships with many African countries; Nigeria is one of the most significant partners for India.

India is the world's fourth largest energy consumer. Since a long time, India was dependent on Middle East countries as the single major source of India's energy imports. India imports 18 per cent from Saudi Arabia, 11 per cent from Iran and 34 per cent of her energy imports comes from other Middle East countries. But from the point of view of energy security, India cannot afford to depend excessively on a single source and needs to diversify her sources for securing energy security. African countries consider India as a key player. They see India as a fast growing economy and want India to invest in their energy and oil sectors along with other major countries of world, most significantly China (CII 2012: pp. 35-38). In recent years India has diversified its crude sources from Middle East countries to African countries. Nigeria has been one of the largest supplier of crude to India among African countries and has become strategically important for India in context of energy security given her rising imports to meet her requirements for energy (MEA 2014: p. 3).

First, India's growing energy needs have forced her to diversify her oil imports. In the past, India has been dependent on West Asia for its oil imports. In recent years, India, like the US and the other major powers, has recognised the energy potential of African countries (Beri 2008).

Second, currently around 24 per cent of India's crude oil imports are sourced from Africa (including North African countries). Indian national oil companies like the Oil and Natural Gas Corporation Videsh Limited (OVL) have invested in equity assets in Sudan, Ivory Coast, Libya, Egypt, and Nigeria, São Tomé and Príncipe Sao Tome Principe Joint Development Area and Gabon.

Third, private sector companies like Reliance have also invested in the oil sector of Sudan. Essar has procured exploration and production blocks in Madagascar and Nigeria. India has recently completed a $ 200 million project to lay a pipeline from Khartoum to Port Sudan on the Red Sea (*Ibid*).

***Co-operation in the Health Segment-Medical and Pharmaceutical Sectors*:** India is one of Nigeria's biggest suppliers of pharmaceuticals. Indian pharmaceutical companies based in Nigeria have imported medical drugs at relatively cheap prices. There has also been a significant increase in Nigerians travelling to India for medical treatment. Nigeria benefits through trade in pharmaceuticals with India and the transfer of medical technology to Nigeria. The inflow of Nigerian patient's to Indian hospitals provides a market for Indian health sector services and also patients from abroad. Constraints like fake drugs are affecting the exports of these companies but these issues are being handled by the governments of India and Nigeria. The Indian High Commissioner in Nigeria used the opportunity to assure Nigerians that India would cooperate with the National Agency for Food and Drug Administration and Control (NAFDAC) to combat fake drugs, that alleged of being originated in India (Alao: SIIA 2011: pp. 12-19).

India and Nigeria are co-operating in the health sector through the treatment of Nigerians in India as well as building local capacity in the health sector in Nigeria. Many Nigerians consider India as the best location to undergo medical treatment. Nigeria has an active engagement with countries like India in the health sectors. As there is a convergence of interest between India and Nigeria in setting up Indian hospitals, transferring technology to local hospitals in Nigeria as well as in the sale of quality and affordable Indian generic drugs to Nigeria is of mutual interest to the two countries (MEA 2012b: p. 2).

***Capacity Building in Education-ICT and IT Sectors*:** During 2012, IT-Association of Nigeria (ITAN) and National Association of Computer and Software Companies of India (NASSCOM), more than 20 leading ICT companies from India have attended the event representing a significant identification with Nigerian government's transformational agenda for the ICT sector and ITAN's new stance to build international partnership to grow the local industry (Tooki: Business World, 2012). Indian ICT firms seek new opportunities in Nigeria. Their investments in ICT in excess of N3 trillion within the last eight years (2005-2012). Nigeria was clearly investors' preferred destination. In line with this, about 20 leading Indian ICT firms came into the country. Indian was seeking new business opportunities in Nigeria's burgeoning ICT industry (Nwachukwu: Business Day 2012).

India has played a significant and beneficial role in Nigeria in the ICT sector. Indian IT professionals are training Nigerians in accountancy and the education sectors. In Nigeria there are several Indian Technologies

Institutes (Vasudevan 2012: p. 5). Many Indian education institutes are famous in Nigeria but NIIT and APTECH are being preferred the most by Nigerian students.

References

Alao, A. (2011), '*Nigeria and the BRICs: Diplomatic, Trade, Cultural and Military Relations*', Occasional Paper No.101, China in Africa Project, November 2011, South African Institute of International Affairs, African perspectives, Global insights.

Beri, R. (2008), '*India and Africa Partnership: Opportunities and Challenges*', IDSA Strategic Comments, New Delhi, 08 April, Available at:<http://www.idsa.in/idsastrategiccomments/India and Africa Partnership_RBeri_080408> (Accessed on 07/12/2012).

Bhaskar, U. (2010), '*Nigeria Gambit Signals India's Africa Strategy*', ONGC Videsh Limited, The International Petroleum Company of India Ltd, Mint: New Delhi, 5 January, Available at: <http://www.ongcvidesh.com/(X(1)S(luco3ny3xk54cuayuvfbfe55))/NewsContent.aspx?ID=378&AspxAutoDetectCookieSupport=1> (Accessed on 05/01/2013).

CII (2012), '*India's Energy Engagement in Africa Engagement in Africa Challenges and Opportunity*', New Delhi.

Focus Africa (2010), '*Sector Profile Nigeria*', Availableat: <http://fofocusafrica.gov.in/Sector_Profile_Nigeria.html> (Accessed on 10/07/2013).

Hoogcarspel, J.A. (2011), '*Securing Natural Resources in a Changing Global Order: The Case of Indo-Nigerian Relation*', MSC, Thesis Political Science, International Relations, Universities Van Amsterdam, Available at:<http://epa.iias.asia/files/Jan%20Arne% 20Hoogcarspel %20%20 Securing%20natural%20resources% 20in%20a%20c hanging%20 global% 20order% 20the%20case%20of% 20Indo-Nigerian%20relations.pdf>(Accessedon 26/02/2013).

Kura, S.B. (2009), '*Nigeria-India Economic, Political and Socio-Cultural Relations: Critical Relations for Continuous Mutual Co-operation,*' IJAPS, Vol. 5, No. 1, January, Available at : < http://ijaps.

usm.my/wpcontent/uploads/2012/06/Sulaiman_ Balarabe_ Kura.pdf> (Accessed on 07/12/2012)

Nwachukwu, I. (2012), '*Exploring Nigeria's Demographic Potential*', Business Day, 26 April, Available at: http://www.business dayonline.com/NG/index.php/markets/investor/36545-exploring-nigerias-demographic-potential (Accessedon 07/02/2013).

Staff, E. (2012), '*Nigeria: Trade and Economic Partnerships*', Afribiz Media, 14 May, Available at: <http://www.afribiz.info/content/nigeria-trade-and-economic-partnerships-2012> (Accessed on 10/07/2013).

The World Bank (2013a), '*Enhancing Capacity to Build ICT-Sector Skills in Africa*', South-South Knowledge Exchange Hub, Available at: <http://wbi.worldbank.org/sske/sske/cases/enhancing-ict-skills-africa>(Accessed on 10/07/2013).

The World Bank (2013b), '*Nigeria Overview*', Nigeria/Data, Context, [Online] Available at: <http://data.worldbank.org/country/nigeria#cp_wdi> (Accessed on 07/12/2012).

Tooki, A. (2012), '*20 Indian IT Companies to Hit Nigeria for Itan / Nascom Summit*', Business World Intelligence, IT World, 17th Monday, Available at: <http://businessworldng.com/web/articles/2439/1/20-Indian-IT-Companies-to-Hit-Nigeria-for—ItanNascom-Summit/Page1.html> (Accessedon 23/05/2013).

Vasudevan, P. (2010), '*The Changing Nature of Nigeria–India Relations*', Programme Paper: AFP2010/02, Chatham House: UK, Available at: <http://www.eisourcebook.org/cms/Dec%202012/The%20Changing%20Nature%20of%20Nigeria India %20Relations.pdf> (Accessed on 20/02/2013).

Vines, A. *et.al* (2009), '*Thirst for African Oil Asian National Oil Companies in Nigeria and Angola*', A Chatham House Report Available at: http://www.chathamhouse.org/sites/default/files/r0809_africanoil.pdf (Accessed on 20/02/2013).

MEA (2014), '*India and Nigeria Relations*', GoI, New Delhi, Available at: < http://www.mea.gov.in/Portal/ForeignRelation/Nigeria_January_ 2014-1.pdf> (Accessed on 12/01/2014).

2

A Focus on Energy Security

This chapter analyses the relationship between India and Nigeria in the context of energy sector. It also tries to provide a brief overview of critical issues in energy security that India faces. As the Indian economy is a growing economy, its need for oil and natural gas is also increasing. In 2011, India was the fourth largest energy consumer in the world after the United States, China and Russia. It was also the fourth largest importer of oil and petroleum products. The country depends heavily on imported crude oil, mostly from the Middle East (EIA 2013). Even though in a slowing global economy, India's energy demand is persistently increasing. In India, demand for energy is more in the transport sector and this will expand in the coming years. On the other hand, India's domestic energy resource base is also insufficient and it is largely dependent on the import of energy resources for its energy use (EIA 2011: p.1). India was the 10th largest economy in the world in 2011, as measured by nominal Gross Domestic Product (GDP). In the International Energy Outlook 2011, EIA projects India and China to account for the biggest share of Asian energy demand growth through 2035 (EIA 2013).

Nigeria is the country with the stock of large amount of crude oil and one of the largest supplier of crude oil to the world among other African countries, after the countries of Middle East. Nigeria is India's strategic partner which supplies crude oil to India; due to this both the countries share a mutual relation which is favourable at both ends (Hoogcarspel 2011: pp. 40-41).

India's Engagement in Africa: Oil Sector

African countries consider India as a key player. They see India as the fasted growing economy and want India to invest in their own energy and oil sector along with other major countries of world, most significantly, China. Indian presence in Africa is favoured by several African countries. Therefore, India needs to carefully undertake its policy towards oil rich African countries according to their mutual needs (CII 2012: pp. 35-38).

China is giving stiff competition to India in energy acquisition in Africa. Table 2.1 below reflects upon

Table 2.1: India's Major Loss to China for Energy Assets Acquisition

Assets	*India's Bidding Companies*	*China's Bidding Company*	*Winner*	*Year*
Sonangol (Angola)	ONGC	Sinopec	China	2004
South Atlantic Petroleum (Nigeria)	OVL (Bid Withdrawn)	CNOOC	China	2006
Heritage Oil 50 per cent stake in Lake Albert Basin (Uganda)	OVL, IOL	CNOOC	China	2009
Bernie Basin(Algeria)	ONGC Led Consortium	CNOOC Consortium	China	2010

Source: CII 2012: p. 39.

India's loss of energy assets acquisition to China. Indian company, Oil and Natural Gas Corporation (ONGC) lost bid to the Chinese company Sinopec in the year 2004 in Angola. Similarly, other Indian companies such as ONGC Videsh Limited (OVL) and Indian Oil Limited (OIL) lost energy assets in Nigeria (2006), in Uganda (2009) and Algeria (2010) to other Chinese companies (*Ibid*: p. 19).

India's Africa Strategy

India is a hydrocarbon deficit country and depends heavily on external supplies. Maintaining the traditional supply from the Gulf, India is in a desperate search for other options overseas. One of the important sources of

Table 2.2: India's Imports of Crude Oil from Africa in 2011-12

Sr. No.	*Country*	*Quantity in (MMT)*
1.	Algeria	2.07
2.	Angola	9.01
3.	Cameroon	0.49
4.	Congo	0.53
5.	Egypt	2.83
6.	Equatorial Guinea	0.9
7.	Equatorial Kenya	0
8.	Gabon	0.14
9.	Ivory Coast	0.17
10.	Libya	0.17
11.	Nigeria	14.13
12.	Sudan	0.69

Source: CII 2012: p. 23.

India's diversification of energy supply is Africa (*Ibid*). Africa's rich hydrocarbon potential adds an entirely new and important dimension to India's ties with the continent. India's growing energy needs have pushed it towards energy cooperation with the African countries (*Ibid*: p. 21).

The Table 2.2 explains India's imports of crude oil from Africa in 2011-12. There are twelve countries in Africa that exports crude oil to India. The country wise export of crude oil is as follows: Algeria (2.07 MMT), Angola (9.01 MMT), Cameroon (0.49 MMT), Congo (0.53 MMT), Egypt (2.83 MMT), Equatorial Guinea (0.9 MMT), Equatorial Kenya (0 MMT), Gabon (0.14 MMT) Ivory Coast (0.17 MMT), Libya (0.17 MMT) and Nigeria (14.13 MMT), Sudan (0.69 MMT).

India's crude oil imports from various countries in Africa in 2011-12 are tabulated below:

India's Petroleum Products Export to Africa

Rivalling China's strategy to secure access to oil and gas blocks in energy rich Africa, India is offering help to oil and gas rich Nigeria to build infrastructure especially power plants. Around 15 per cent of the crude oil imports to India come from Nigeria. Nigeria has 36.2 billion barrels per day of proven oil resources and is a member of the Organisation of Petroleum Exporting Countries (OPEC) (Bhaskar:–ONGC 2010: pp. 1-3). According to the International Energy Agency, India will become the third largest oil importer after the U.S. and China before 2025, with its energy demands expected to almost double by 2030 (*Ibid*).

India has only 0.7 per cent of the world's total oil reserves with a Reserve/Production (R/P) ratio of 30 years. While it produces 38.9 Million Tons (MT), it consumes 155.5 MT or 3.9 per cent of the total global consumption, making India the world's fourth largest

Table 2.3: India's Petroleum Products Export to Africa

	Value ($ MN)			*Share Imports to Africa (%)*		
	2008-09	*2009-10*	*2010-11*	*2008-09*	*2009-10*	*2010-11*
Total Export	185295.5	178751.4	252354.3	-	-	-
Export to Africa	14813.8	13432.9	21055.0	100.0	100.0	100.0
Petroleum Products	3242.9	2843.1	490.07	21.9	21.2	23.3

Source: FICC 2011: p. 14.

oil consumer. Currently the country is importing 75 per cent of its total oil consumption, which is further expected to increase to 90 per cent by 2025 (CII 2012: pp. 1-2).

The Table 2.3 explains India's petroleum products exports to Africa. The petroleum products share of imports to Africa is growing. In 2008-09, it was 21.9 per cent and in 2010-11 it reached to 23.3 per cent. This trade relationship between India and Nigeria shows that India's major energy assets are in Nigerian oil companies and India can look at Nigeria as a thriving investment destination.

Table 2.4: Indian Oil Companies in Africa

Country	*Indian Companies*	*Type of Investment*	*Size of Investment*
Cote d'Ivoire	Unknown (various companies acting as a consortium)	Oil Prospecting	US$ 1 billion
Nigeria	NTPC	LNG	US$ 1.7 billion
Nigeria	IOC	Oil Refinery	US$ 3.5 billion
Nigeria	IOC	LNG Plant and Oil Refinery	US$ 2-4 billion
Sudan	Videocon Group	Oil Prospecting	US$ 1 00 million (76% stake)

Source: Cheru and Obi 2010: p. 38.

The Table 2.4 explains that there are various Indian oil companies having projects in Africa. Indian companies have invested in Nigeria, Cote d'Ivoire and Sudan. These companies invested in Nigeria's oil sector and in various aligned activities. They also invested in National Thermal Power Corporation (NTPC). The investment of Indian companies in Liquefied Natural

Chart: 2.1: India's Oil Production and Consumption

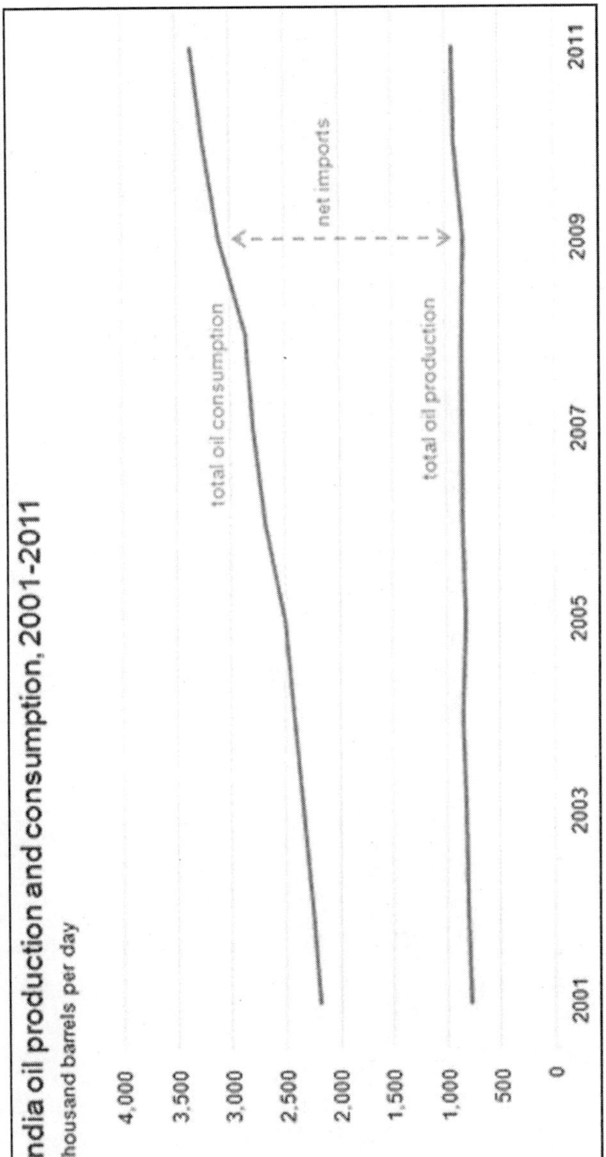

Source: ETAUS Energy Information Administration International Energy Statistics: India 2013.

Table 2.5: India's Major Successful Energy Projects in Africa

No.	*Country*	*Blocks*	*Participating Interest and Partners*
1.	Libya	Block 86	Oil (50%) Operator and IOCL (50%)
		102/4	Oil (50%) Operator and IOC (50%)
		Area 95/96	Oil (25%) IOCL (25%) and SIPEX (50%)
		Contract Area - 43	OVL (100%)
2.	Sudan	GNOP Block 1, 2 and 4	OVL (25%), CNPC (40%), PETRONAS (30%), Sudapet (5%) Joint –Operatorship.
		Block 5 A	OVL (24.125%) PETRONAS (67.875%) PETRONAS and Sudapet are Joint Venture
		Pipeline Project	OVL (90%), OIL (10%)
3.	Nigeria	OPL-279 and OPL- 285	OVL hold PI through its JV ONGC Mittal Energy Limited (OMEL), which is the Pre-Tour of these two Offshore Blocks. Other Partners are Total and EMO OPL-279: OMEL (45.5%) EMO (40%) total (14.5%) OPL-285: OMEL (64.33%), EMO (10%) total – (25.67%).
		OPL- 205 (Onshore)	25% Equity of Sunterra Nigeria 205 Limited, which is Nigerian Company having 70% Interest in Exploration Block OPL 205.
		OPL – 226	Essar Energy (100%)

(Contd.)

(Contd. Table 2.5)

No.	*Country*	*Blocks*	*Participating Interest and Partners*
4.	Egypt	Block 3 and 4 Offshore	Block 3 (South Quseir) is Located in Red Sea Area and Block 4 (South Sinai) at the Junction of Gulf of Suez and Red Sea GSPC. Led Consortium was awarded these two blocks in GANOPE international bid round 2008. GSPC (50% operator), Oil (25%), HPCL (25%) – PSA not signed.
5.	Gabon	SHAKTI	OIL (45% Operator), OIC (45%) Marvis Pvt Ltd. (10%)
6.	Mozambique	Offshore Area 1	Anadarko (36.5% Operator) Mitsui E.P. Mozambique Area 1 (20%), BPRL Venture Mozambique Rovuma 1 (10%) and Cove Energy Mozambique Rovuma Offshore (8.5%), Empresa Nacional de Hydrocarbonetos (ENH), E.P. (15%).
7.	Madagascar	2 Onshore Blocks in the Morondava Basin	Essar Energy (100%).

Source: CII 2012: pp. 27-29.

Gas (LNG) is around $ 1.7 billion. Indian Oil Corporation (IOC) invested in oil refinery around $ 3.5 billion. The IOC also invested in LNG plant and oil which is around $ 2-4 billion (*Ibid*: p. 38).

Chart 2.1 explains India's oil production and consumption during 2001-2011. As per US Energy Information Administration (EIA) international energy statistics, the production of Indian oil varies with small difference, but from 2001 onwards the consumption of oil in India has increased. In 2011, the consumption was very high as compared to the year 2001 or even the year 2009. According to the US EIA, international energy statistics that, the consumption is increasing because of the increase demand of oil in India.

India's Major Successful Energy Projects in Africa

Since several years, India is involved in Africa's oil sector. In this region, Indian companies have built many projects. Indian Oil Companies have invested in equity assets, Gabon, Ivory Coast, Kenya, Libya, Nigeria and Nigeria Sao Tome Principe Joint Development Zone, Sudan and Tunisia (CII 2012: p. 24). The following Table 2.5 explains Indian companies' involvement in oil sector in various African countries.

India's Investment in Renewable Energy Sources in Africa

India has offered to spend and strengthen its cooperation with the African countries in the field of renewable energy. India is already assisting African countries for electrification of village through solar energy and aim to set up 40 solar charging stations and 40 biomass gasifiers. India has also started many institutes which have tailor made training programmes in various areas of renewable energy. India is ready to share her experience, knowledge and technology in the field of renewable energy with African countries (CII: 2012: pp. 31-34).

India had offered $ five billion for the next three year under line of credit and $ 700 million as assistance to help Africa achieve its developments goals. The drive to increase energy access in Africa has helped accelerate the deployment of renewable energy source. It is required to import much of the renewable power generation equipment. This will provide good business opportunities for India's growing partnership with countries of Africa in the energy sector and it is a part of its conscious policy to develop South-South Co-operation (*Ibid*: pp. 31-34).

India Seeks Greater Participation in Hydrocarbon Sector in Africa

Africa can play a major role to meet its growing demand for crude oil and gas in the years ahead. Addressing the media on the eve of Third India-Africa Hydrocarbons Conference in New Delhi, the Minister of State for Petroleum and Natural Gas Shri R.P.N. Singh stated that "India sought to expand its presence across the hydrocarbon value chain in Africa. With Africa's economic development picking up momentum and its energy demands increasing, India is also poised to become a dependable supplier of petroleum products to Africa. India-Africa Hydrocarbons Conference has been conceptualised with the objective to foster bilateral trade relations in the hydrocarbon sector, understand policy and regulatory frameworks and offer opportunities for investment in upstream and downstream sector of the two regions" (PIB, GOI 2011).

With India's foreign policy focussing on partnering with Africa, the Ministry of Petroleum and Natural Gas in collaboration with FICCI, has initiated the India-Africa Hydrocarbons Conference as an institutional mechanism.

The Third India-Africa Hydrocarbons Conference, scheduled to be held at The Grand, New Delhi on 9-10 December, 2011 focuses on:

1. Opportunities for boosting India-Africa trade in oil and gas;

2. Prospects of Indian investment in Africa's upstream and downstream sectors;

3. Policy and regulatory frameworks of Africa and India: and

4. Co-operation in capacity building in Africa through human resource development, transfer of technology, research and development.

India is the world's fourth largest oil importer, with oil and gas constitutes 45 per cent of the country's primary energy basket (oil 35 per cent and natural gas 10 per cent). About 78 per cent of India's petroleum consumption is met from crude oil imports, while about 25 per cent of natural gas consumption also comes from imports. To meet this growing demand for crude oil and gas in India, Africa is expected to play a major role in the years ahead. India's refining capacity, which is 194 million tonnes per annum, is set to increase to 238 million tonnes by 2013. This means an additional need of 40 million tonnes of crude per annum. The current demand for gas at 166 Million Metric Standard Cubic Meter per Day (MMSCMD) is projected to go up to 443 MMSCMD by 2017 (*Ibid*, 2011).

India has been following a policy of consciously diversifying its sources of crude oil imports so as to reduce its dependence on any particular region of the world. Today, 21.5 per cent (35.3 million tonnes per annum as against 22 million tonnes in 2004-05) of India's crude oil imports come from Africa, with the major suppliers being Algeria, Angola, Cameroon, Egypt, Equatorial Guinea, Nigeria and Sudan. India is keen to participate in the exploration and production opportunities in the upstream sector of Algeria, Angola, Chad, Congo, Cote D'Ivoire, Gabon, Ghana, Mozambique, Nigeria, Sudan, Tanzania, Uganda etc. India's companies are also interested in farm-in opportunities in gas-producing blocks, especially in Algeria, Egypt, Libya, and Nigeria. Today, India's oil companies are present in around 24 countries (*Ibid,* 2011).[1]

The Government is encouraging National Oil Companies to aggressively pursue equity oil; Indian oil companies are present in around 24 countries[2] with a total investment by oil (Power Supply Unit (PSUs), OVL, OIL, IOCL, Hindustan Petroleum Corporation Limited (HPCL), Gas Authority of India Limited (GAIL) and Bharat Petroleum Corporation Limited (BPCL) alone of Rs 64,832 crore.[2] In the downstream sector of Africa, Indian oil companies are operating in Egypt, Kenya, Mauritius, Uganda and Tanzania. India seeks to expand its presence across the hydrocarbon value chain in Africa. Over the last two editions, the India-Africa Hydrocarbons Conference has played an important role in creating a better understanding of the capabilities of India and Africa in the field of oil and gas. It has offered immense opportunities to the stakeholders in the hydrocarbon sector to interact and discuss potential tie-ups in the form of equity investments, project management, joint venture, technology transfer, up-gradation of oil and gas infrastructure facilities, development and management of technical skills and human resources and supply of equipment and consultancy services (*Ibid*, 2011).

Nigeria's and Other Africa Countries

Nigeria's New Vision:– Oil and Gas Sector

Nigeria is still working towards expanding one of its valuable resources that is hydrocarbon. Hence, the medium term programme with regard to oil and gas sector will motivate investments in upstream as well as downstream by inspiring the local and foreign investment in the sector of new refineries and advancing local value addition to uphold the consumption of local resources i.e., in terms of materials and human resources. The Nigeria's New Vision: 2020, will focus on various aspects namely; increase in crude oil refining capacity, its oil and gas reserves and expanding exports that will take into account the refined petroleum products and other directives from oil and gas (Nigeria Vision: 2020, 2010: p.72).

Objectives, Targets and Strategies to be Achieved Regarding Oil and Gas Sector in Nigeria (2010-2013).

There have been various objectives to be achieved during the period between the years 2010-2013 in the sector of oil and gas which are as follows:

Objectives

In Nigeria's Vision :2020 the objectives for the period of 2010-13 are mentioned below:

1. To transform the national oil company into a world class, commercially driven and globally competitive organisation;

2. To increase local refining capacity to serve both domestic and original markets;

3. To ensure provision of adequate funding for oil and gas projects; and

4. To develop Nigeria's gas industry, separate from the oil industry while delivering significant capacity additions to serve local and export gas markets.

Targets

The major targets under Vision: 2020 are:

1. To grow reserves from 36.5 billion barrels by 2010 and 50 billion barrels by 2013;

2. Grow crude oil production capacity from 1.8million barrels per day (MBPD) to 3.2 mbpd by 2010 and 4.5 mbpd by 2013; and

3. To grow National Oil Corporation (NOC) production to over 250,000 barrels-per-day (bpd) in 2013.

Strategies

Several strategies are being taken to give Vision: 2020. Major strategies are explained in brief below. These are:

1. Invest in and embark on aggressive exploration for oil reserves and production in all parts of the country;

2. Provide appropriate fiscal incentives to attract investments in oil exploration, at the same time ensuring reasonable returns for the nation;

3. Develop the NOC into medium oil and producing company that can operate internationally;

4. Intensify human capital development in NOC to create an enabling environment to attract foreign and local investment in refineries;

5. Complete structural and legal reform in oil and gas targets at creating an efficient, transparent and commercially viable industry; and

Gas Vision: A vibrant gas sector developed in comprehensive and integrated manner in order to accelerate in growth of the economy (*Ibid*: pp. 92-95).

Nigeria's Share in Africa's Oil Reserves

Africa accounted for eight per cent of the world's proven oil reserves and 7.8 per cent of the world's total natural gas. Africa produced 417.4 million tons of oil and consumed 158.3 million tonnes, in 2011 (CII 2012: p. 15).

Table 2.6: Development of Crude Oil Reserves 2001-2011

Country	*At End 2001*	*At End 2010*	*At End 2011*			
	Thousand Million Barrels	*Thousand Million Barrels*	*Thousand Million Barrels*	*Thousand Million Barrels*	*Share of Total*	*R/P Ratio*
Algeria	11.3	12.2	1.5	12.2	0.7%	19.3
Angola	6.5	13.5	1.8	13.5	0.8%	21.2
Chad	0.9	1.5	0.2	1.5	0.1%	36.1
Republic of Congo (Brazzaville)	1.6	1.9	0.3	1.9	0.1%	18.0
Egypt	3.7	4.5	0.6	4.3	0.3%	16.0
Equatorial Guinea	1.1	1.7	0.2	1.7	0.1%	18.5
Gabon	2.4	3.7	0.5	3.7	0.2%	41.2
Libya	36.0	47.1	6.1	47.1	2.9%	*

(Contd.)

(Contd. Table 2.6)

Country	At End 2001 Thousand Million Barrels	At End 2010 Thousand Million Barrels	At End 2011			
			Thousand Million Barrels	Thousand Million Barrels	Share of Total	R/P Ratio
Nigeria	31.5	37.2	5.0	37.2	2.3%	41.5
Sudan and South Sudan	0.7	6.7	0.9	6.7	0.4%	40.5
Tunisia	0.5	0.4	0.1	0.4	◆	15.0
Other Africa	0.6	2.3	0.3	2.2	0.1%	27.0
Total Africa	96.8	132.7	17.6	132.4	8.0%	41.2

Note: ◆ less than 0.05 per cent. * More than 100 years.
Source: BP Statistical Review of World Energy, 2012: p. 6.

The Table 2.6 explain the development of crude oil reserves in different African countries in 2001-2011. According to this table, Nigeria's development of crude oil reserves at end of 2001 was 31.5 thousand million barrels. At end of 2010 it was 37.2 thousand million barrels, and by 2011 it was 5.0 thousand million barrels and share of total was 2.3 per cent. Nigeria's R/P ratio was 41.5 (*Ibid*: pp. 19-20).

Recoveries in the oil exporting economies like Angola, Chad, Equatorial Guinea, Gabon and Nigeria in 2010 are an outcome of the strengthening of external demand and oil prices. Africa is emerging as a major source of energy supplies. The countries of North Africa, such as Algeria, Libya and Nigeria in West Africa were already principal oil producing countries over the past decades; but the African continent as a whole has come to be seen as a global oil and gas producer, only in the last few years. Major oil and gas reserves are available in Angola, Brazzaville, Congo, Gabon and Nigeria particularly in the deep offshore waters (Exim Bank of India, 2011: p.1).

Nigeria holds the largest natural gas reserves in Africa, in addition to oil, but there are challenges in the production process due to limited infrastructure, where countries like India can assist. Natural gas that is associated with oil production is mostly flared till now, but the development of regional pipelines, the expansion of LNG infrastructure, and policies to ban gas flaring are expected to accelerate growth in the sector, both for export and domestic use in electricity generation (EIA, 2012).

Given the vast resources of crude oil, Nigeria is a natural choice for India for hydrocarbon imports. Nigeria and India's relationship has been strengthened by the two India-Africa Forum Summits of 2008 and 2011.

This has in turn given a boost to trade and commerce with countries in Africa such as Nigeria.

India-Africa Forum Summits

There were two summits till date held between India and Africa. The First Forum Summit was held in 2008 in New Delhi and the second was held in 2011 in Addis Ababa. The first summit of 2008 recognised that energy and infrastructure is fundamental to the economic growth of developing countries and acknowledges that infrastructural development and environmental sustainability are some of the priority areas of the New Economic Partnership for Africa's Development (NEPAD).

Africa and India agreed to place energy, infrastructure and environmental sustainability as one of the key areas of co-operation and committed themselves to the following areas:

1. *Development of public-private partnerships in infrastructure development;*

2. *Co-operation in the development of transport and telecommunications networks;*

3. *Co-operation in the field of exploration and exploitation of natural resources, as well as value addition;*

4. *Creation of enabling environment for investment and development of renewable and non-renewable energy sources;*

5. *Co-operation and capacity-building in best practices and adaptation on the impact of climate change and desertification;*

6. *Exchange of experiences on recent advances on alternative energy sources and sustainable land management;*

7. Development of co-operation in fibre optic cables construction around and within Africa for broadband access network specifically for landlocked countries; and

8. Technical co-operation for Clean Development Mechanism (CDM) (IAFS, 2008).

9. In 2011, note that India has actively engaged with Africa through the India/Africa Hydrocarbon Conferences and welcomes India's commitment to work with Africa to process its resources including by establishing refineries in some countries;

10. Define together with the Renewable Energy Certificate System (RECs) the regional power pools and national governments concrete projects in the field of hydropower, wind and bio-energy in African countries, which have high potential; and

11. Co-operation to explore renewable sources of energy in Africa (IAFS 2011).

Africa is full of natural resources, therefore, India is looking towards Nigeria as a strategically important continent.

India's Oil Strategy in Nigeria

India persistently aims to build up energy security with Nigeria at competitive prices. There have been various policies laid down with regard to fossil fuels such as; "policy promoting increased domestic production, a policy promoting the acquisition of equity in foreign oil and gas companies by private and national oil companies and a policy to create strategic reserves" (Hoogcarspel, 2011: pp. 40-41).

According to Hoogcarspel, Jan Arne:

The risk of oil disruptions from Nigeria increases, but the risks are spread and mitigated. If India manages to increase supplies from sources other than the Middle East, it could increase its energy security by spreading the risks. Indo-Nigerian relations are conducted in a situation of increasing energy scarcity. Demand is growing, stocks are dwindling and reserves are not evenly distributed geographically. India is particularly lacking in oil reserves, but dependence on foreign gas and coal reserves is growing as well. The success of India's energy security strategy is partly determined by the development of the energy situation. The demand side of this situation is influenced by factors such as population growth, rising per capita income, technological changes and Indian policy (*Ibid*).

Nigeria offers an ideal partnership for promoting India's energy security strategy with its proven oil reserves and a major exporter of crude oil to various countries across the global.

Nigeria's Crude Oil and Condensate Exports

Europe is the largest regional importer of Nigerian oil. In 2012, Europe imported 889,000 bbl/d of crude oil and condensate from Nigeria, accounting for 44 per cent of total Nigerian exports. In the same year, Nigeria exported between 2.2 million to 2.3 million bbl/d of crude oil and condensate, according to an analysis of data from Euro Stat, APEX Tanker Data, and FACTS Global Energy. The United States has been the largest importer of Nigerian crude oil for at least the past decade. In 2012, the United States imported 406,000 bbl/d of crude oil from Nigeria, accounting for 18 per cent of Nigeria's total exports.[3] India (12 per cent), Brazil (8 per cent), Spain (8 per cent), and the Netherlands (7 per cent) made up the remaining top five largest recipients of Nigerian oil (EIA, 2013).

India's Energy Assets in Nigeria

Table 2.7 below explains India's energy assets in Nigeria. Indian companies also run some joint ventures

Chart 2.2: Nigeria's Crude Oil and Condensate

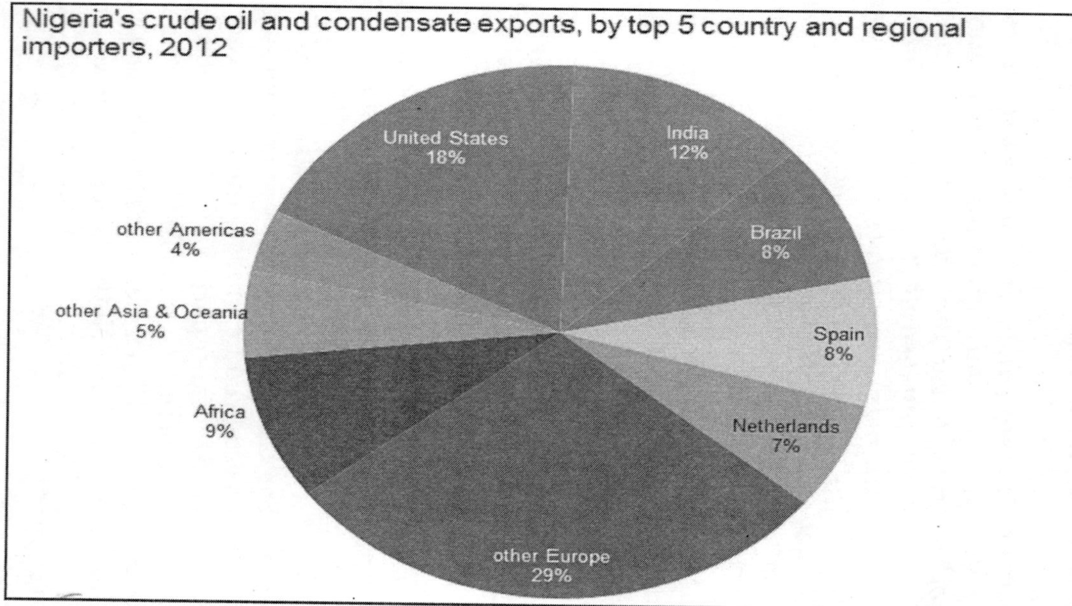

Source: EIA: Nigeria, 2013.

Table 2.7: India's Energy Assets in Nigeria

No.	*Country*	*Name of Assets*	*Indian Company*	*Remarks*
1.	Nigeria	Block 279	OMEL (JV of OVL and Mittal Investment SARL)	P.I. 60% of Offshore Deep Water
		Block 285	OMEL	P.I. 90 % of Offshore Deep Water
		Block 297	OMEL	P.I. 40 % of Offshore Deep Water
	Sao Tome and Principe (Joint Development Zone)	Exploration of Block –II	OVL	P.I. 13.5% with Equator Exploration Co.

(Contd.)

(Contd. Table 2.7)

No.	*Country*	*Name of Assets*	*Indian Company*	*Remarks*
		OPL Block 226	Essar Energy	Block Withdrawn, Decision Being Reviewed for Offer
		OPL 2005-06	Sterling oil	Under Discussion
		Setting up of a Refinery – talks Underway	IOC and Essar	MOU Signed
	Equatorial Guinea	Setting up of 2x250 MC Coal Based Power Plant in Nigeria	NTPC	Expressed Interested in Securing 23% Stake of M/S Devon Energy
		Block EG 12 and 13	OVL	

with Equatorial Guinea and Sao Tome for assisting their projects in Nigeria. In Nigeria, India's assets include block 279 by ONGC Mittal Energy Ltd (OMEL).

Bilateral Relations between India and Nigeria

In Africa, Nigeria is the largest trading partners of India and also the largest market in Africa for Indian exports. In the first quarter of 2012, India dislocated USA as Nigeria's largest trading partner (FICCI, 2011: p. 2). Both the countries have benefitted greatly by sharing resources and experience. For India, Nigeria is the second most important supplier of crude oil (India Africa Connect, 2010).

The Table 2.8 depicts India's exports to Nigeria and its imports from Nigeria in numerical data. The imports as well as exports were growing since 2003, but in 2009-10 both had shown a downturn because of factors such as the global financial crisis of 2008. Now, Nigeria is engaged in the exercise for reforming the oil and gas industry which is governed by laws formed more than 40 years ago. The aim is to inject more transparency, reduce arbitrariness, promote fiscal responsibility and insulate the entire oil and gas industry from political influence so that it acts as catalyst for the economic renaissance of the country (India Africa Connect, 2010).

Nigeria is one of the largest African partners of India. Bilateral trade between the two was over USD$ 10 billion in 2009, making India the second largest trading partner of Nigeria. The trade surplus of USD$ 7 billion that Nigeria enjoyed last year was nearly a fifth of its global trade surplus. The foreign exchange earned by Nigeria contributes to the development of infrastructure and improvements in the lives of Nigerians. Nigeria is becoming a favourite destination for Indian investors in areas as diverse as petroleum, power, health, transport, bio-fuels and tele-communication training (*Ibid*).

Table 2.8: The Rising Trend in the Bilateral Trade

No.	*Country*	*2003-04*	*2004-05*	*2005-06*	*2006-07*	*2007-08*	*2008-09*	*2009-10*
1.	Indian Export to Nigeria	565.49	644.68	874.03	903.48	1083.34 (20% growth)	1529.26 (41% y-o-y growth)	1408.25 (-8 %)
2.	Indian Imports from Nigeria	75.64*	48.40*	72.46*	7026.93	7616.09 (8.47% growth)	8900.35 (14.1% y-o-y growth)	7287.91 (-18%)

Note (*) Oil Import

Source: MEA 2012b: p. 03.

To promote trade relations between the two countries, more specifically in the hydrocarbons sector several high level delegations have taken place between India and Nigeria.

Bilateral visits during 2012 and first half of 2013 for the promotion of Hydrocarbons were as follows:

1. A delegation led by Governor of Borno visited India in September 2012. He met Minister for Renewable Energy, among others then Vice President of Nigeria, Dr Goodluck Jonathan visited India from November 4-7, 2007 to attend the Federalism Conference. A high level delegation attended India–Africa Hydrocarbon Conference from November 6–7, 2007. Shri Anand Sharma, Minister for Commerce and Industry visited Nigeria on 15-17 January 2010 to attend the 'Namaskar Africa' event jointly organised by FICCI;

2. Murli Deora, Minister for Petroleum and Natural Gas paid a bilateral visit to Nigeria from 25-26 January, 2010;

3. On May 7, 2011, R. P. N. Singh, Minister of State (MOS) (Petroleum and Natural Gas) paid a courtesy call on Nigerian President Dr Goodluck Jonathan in Abuja to deliver Hon'ble PM's letter of invitation for the second Africa India Forum Summit; and

4. Commissioner for Economic Affairs of African Union (AU) participated in the Partnership Summit 2008 in March 2008 and spoke on "Ensuring Growth, Making it Inclusive: The West Asian and African Views." Deputy Chairperson of AUC, Commissioner for Trade and Industry and Commissioner for Infrastructure and Energy participated in the India Africa Forum Summit in April 2008 (MEA 2012 b: pp.1-2).

5. A four-member delegation led by Nigerian Minister for Power Prof Chindedu Nebo visited New Delhi December 7-9, 2013 to have interaction with BHEL for strengthening Nigeria's power sector.

6. Secretary, Department of Heavy Industry, GOI, Sutanu Behuria, accompanied by P. K. Uppal, Executive Director, BHEL, visited Abuja, Nigeria to explore co-operation in power sector (MEA 2014: p. 2).

To strengthen this bilateral relationship several initiatives has been taken. One of them is the extension of lines of credits (LOC's) to Nigeria through the Exim Bank of India.

Indian Lines of Credit (LOCs) to Nigeria

Exim Bank of India has placed special emphasis on extension of LOCs as an effective market entry mechanism with particular focus on small and medium enterprises. It extends LOCs to overseas financial institutions, regional development banks, sovereign governments and other entities overseas, to enable buyers in those countries to import developmental and infrastructural projects, equipment, goods and services from India, on deferred credit terms. Indian exporters can obtain payment of eligible value from Exim Bank, without recourse to them, against negotiation of shipping documents. Exim Bank also extends LOCs at the behest of Government of India. Exim Bank's LOCs[4] afford a risk-free, non-recourse export financing option to Indian exporters.[4] It has now in place 143 Lines of Credit, covering over 73 countries in Africa, Asia, Latin America, Europe, Oceania and the Commonwealth of Independent States (CIS), with credit commitments of over $ 6.89 billion, available for financing exports from India established primarily to enhance Indian exports to developing countries. LOC have become an effective tool for market penetration and a stepping stone to unchartered territories of Africa and Latin America (Exim Bank of India, 2007: p. 8).

Exim Bank has extended a LOC of $ five million to the Nigerian Export Import Bank (NEXIMB). This LOC is extended for supply of capital and engineering goods, industrial manufactures, consumer durables, commodities and services from India. Under the LOC to NEXIMB, importers based in Nigeria will make advance payment of 10 per cent of contract value and Exim Bank will provide credit for 90 per cent of contract value to NEXIMB. Exim Bank will reimburse Indian exporters upfront upon the shipment of goods and provision of services. Exim Bank's LOC to Neximbank will help strengthen India's trade relations with Nigeria (*Ibid*: p. 7).

Table 2.9: Exim Bank's Pipeline LOCs (Updated as of January 14, 2013)

No.	*Borrower*	*Purpose*	*Credit Amount ($ MN)*
1.	Government of Nigeria	Various Projects in Nigeria	100.00

Source: Exim Bank of India 2013.

Notes: The above table lists LOCs where offers have been made by the Exim Bank to the recipient governments and their designated agencies but the offer has not yet been accepted and/or the LOC Agreements are yet to be signed. As such, this list is only for information of future possible LOCs and does not tantamount to a commitment by Exim Bank. The validity of the above details is contingent upon the acceptance of the offers by the LOC recipients and the subsequent signing of the LOC Agreement (Exim Bank of India, 2013).

The Table 2.9 shows the Government of Nigeria borrower credit from Exim Bank for purpose of investment in various project in Nigeria on 14, January

2013. The Government of Nigeria borrowed $100.00 mn credit amounts.

As Nigerian oil sector is growing rapidly, the Indian energy policy towards Nigeria is also changing. Their importance and involvement is being discussed below:

Involvement and Importance of Nigeria in India's Energy Policy

India's interest in Nigeria's oil sector has three components:

1. Term contract for crude purchase;
2. Participation in the upstream sector; and
3. Refineries.

In 2005 there were several significant developments in India and Nigeria hydrocarbons co-operation. An Inter-Ministerial Task Force of the Government of India visited Nigeria in November 2005 which resulted in a Memorandum of Understanding (MOU) between ONGC-Mittal Energy Ltd. and the Nigerian government for a $ 6 billion oil infrastructure deal. Indian companies are placed to do well in the next Nigerian oil licensing round of 45 blocks that Abuja announced on 3 April, 2007 (Singh 2007: p. 4).

Challenges

1. The Success of these Policy Initiatives is Influenced

2. The degree to which India can integrate its fragmented energy policy; and

3. The degree to which the Indian government can deliver on its promises and the financial autonomy of state-owned corporations.

The role of Nigeria in India's energy policy is basically a strategy for the diversification of suppliers and the overall need to gain increasing access to foreign reserves (Hoogcarspel 2011: pp. 40-41).

3. Other Issues that have Aroused India's Interest in Nigerian Oil Reserves are:

(a) The transportation of supplies does not cross any major oil checkpoints;

(b) Nigerian oil is sweet;

(c) Nigeria and India have an established relationship on which future relations can be built; and

(d) Trade with the Middle East could become troublesome due to Hindu nationalist rhetoric in India and Nigerian reserves have increased significantly between 1990 and 2010 (*Ibid*).

Conclusion

Nigeria plays an important role in Indian economy due to its crude oil exports to India. In this chapter the relationship between Nigeria and India with regard to the energy sector has been analysed. With the public sector, the private companies also play an important role in share of world crude oil reserves in India. Africa is endowed with natural resources such as hydrocarbons and India is looking forward to it as energy hub for its growing energy needs. In this strategy, Nigeria occupies a central role as the largest supplier of crude oil to India. New initiatives, such as India-Africa Summits between India and Africa are efforts towards establishing a healthy relationship. Oil producing countries like Nigeria, where the economy is heavily dependent on oil sector, new initiatives outlined in its vision document 20:2020, aims to grow Nigeria's market share in the world economy and in this strategy India is a favoured destination for their exports of crude hydrocarbons.

References

Bhaskar, U. (2010), *'Nigeria Gambit Signals India's Africa Strategy'*, ONGC Videsh Limited, The International Petroleum Company of India, Ltd, Mint: New Delhi, 5 January, Available at: <http://www.ongcvidesh.com/(X(1)S(luco3ny3xk 54cuayuvfbfe 55)) /NewsContent. aspx?ID=378&AspxAuto Detect Cookie Support =1> (Accessed on 05/01/2013).

B. P. Statistical Review of World Energy (2012), Available at:<http://www.bp.com/assets/bp_internet/globalbp/globalbp_uk_english/reports_and_publications/statistical_ energy_review_2011/STAGING/local_assets/pdf/statistical_review_ of_world _energy_full_report_2012. pdf>(Accessed on 26/02/2013).

Cheru, F. and Obi, C. (2010), *The Rise of China and India in Africa: Challenges, Opportunities and Critical Interventions*, New York: Nordic Africa Institute.

CII (2012), 'India's Energy Engagement in Africa Challenges and Opportunity', New Delhi, Available at: < http://www.cii.in/> (Accessed on 07/01/3013).

EIA (2013), *'India Background, Country Analysis Briefs'*, Available at: <http://www.eia.gov/EMEU/cabs/India/pdf.pdf> (Accessed on 018/03/2013)).

EIA (2013), *'Nigeria Background, Country Analysis Briefs'*, Available at: <http://www.eia.gov/countries/cab.cfm?fips= IN> (Accessed on 030/12/2013).

Exim Bank (2007), *'Exim Bank's Operative Lines of Credit'*, Export-Import Bank of India, Available at: <http://www.exim bankindia. com/loc.asp> (Accessed on 26/02/2013).

Exim Bank (2011), *'Eximius: Export Advantage'*, Export Import Bank of India, Available at: http://www.eximbank india.com/eamar11.pdf (Accessed on 26/02/2013).

Exim Bank (2013), *'Exim Bank's Pipeline LOCs'*, Export-Import Bank of India, Available at: http://www.eximbankindia. com/locpipeline.pdf (Accessed on 26/02/2013).

FICCI (2011), *'Background Paper on India--Africa Business Partnership Summit'*, Ministry of Commerce and Industry, Ministry of External Affairs, Government of India, Knowledge Partner Exim Bank, October 12-13, HICC, Hyderabad, India, Available at:<http://www.ficci.com/events/20776/ISP/IABP-Background-paper.pdf>(Accessed on- 07/12/2012).

Hoogcarspel, J.A. (2011), Securing Natural Resources in a Changing Global Order: The Case of Indo-Nigerian Relations. MSC, Thesis Political Science, International Relations, Universities Van Amsterdam. pp: 40-41, Available- at: <http://epa.iias.asia/files/Jan%20Arne%20Hoogcarspel %20%20Securing %20natural%20resources%20in% 20a%20changing 20global% 20order%20the%20case%20of%20Indo-Nigerian% 20relations.pdf> (Accessed26/02/2013).

IAFS (2008), *'Plan of Action of the Framework for Co-operation on the India Africa Forum Summit'*, Addis Ababa, Embassy of India: First IAFS, April 8-9, New Delhi, Available at: <http://www.indianembassy.gov.et/?q=node/21> (Accessed on 26/02/2013).

IAFS (2011), *'Plan of Action of the Framework for Co-operation on the India Africa Forum Summit'*, Addis Ababa, Embassy of India: Second IAFS, 25th May, New Delhi, Available at: <http://www.indianembassy.gov.et/?q=node/21> (Accessed on 26/02/2013).

India Africa Connect (2010), 'Indo-Nigeria Bilateral Relation', Indo Asian News Service, Available at: <http://www.indiaafricaconnect.in/index.php?param=news/2295/business-industry/107> (Accessed on 27/05/2013).

MEA (2012b), 'India Nigeria Relations', Government of India, New Delhi, Available at:<http://www.mea.gov.in/Images/pdf/Nigeria-January-2012.pdf>(Accessed on 26/02/2013).

Nigeria Vision 20:2020 (2010), 'The First National Implementation Plans (2010-2013)', Vol. II: Sectoral Plans and Programmes, Available at:<http://www.npc.gov.ng/vault/files/NV2020-NIP-Volume-II-Original —document_edited__versioin3_10_06_2010.pdf> (Accessed on 07/12/2012).

PIB (2011), '*India Seek Greater Participation in Hydrocarbon Sector in Africa*', Government of India, Available at: http://pib.nic.in/newsite/erelease.aspx?relid=78162 (Accessed on 22/03/2013).

Singh, S. K. (2007), '*India and West Africa: Burgeoning Relationship*', Africa Programme/Asia Programme Briefing Paper AFP/ASPBP, Chatham House, 07 January, Available at:-http://www.chathamhouse.org/sites/default/files/public/Research/Africa/bpindiawestafrica0407.pdf (Accessed on 07/12/2012).

MEA (2014), '*India and Nigeria Relations*', GoI, New Delhi, Available at: <http://www.mea.gov.in/Portal/ForeignRelation/Nigeria_January_2014-1.pdf>(> (Accessdon12/01/2014).

Footnotes

1. Australia, Brazil, Cuba, Colombia, Egypt, Gabon, Iraq, Iran, Kazakhstan, Libya, Myanmar, Mozambique, Nigeria, Nigeria Sao Tome Principe, Oman, Russia, Sudan, Syria, Trinidad and Tobago, Timor-Leste, Vietnam, Venezuela and Yemen (PIB, GOI 2011).

3. Nigeria's high-quality light, sweet crude is a preferred gasoline feedstock, in 2011, United States imports of Nigerian crude have decreased in volume and as a share of total imports, with the trend continuing in 2012. According to EIA, although total crude imports into the United States are falling, imports from Nigeria has declined at a steeper rate. The main reasons underlying this trend are that some Gulf Coast refiners have reduced Nigerian imports in favour of domestically-produced crude, and that two refineries in the U.S. East Coast, which were significant buyers of Nigerian crude, were idled in late 2011. As a result, Nigerian crude as a share of total United States imports has fallen to five per cent in the first half of 2012, down from 10 and 11 per cent in the first half of 2011 and 2010, respectively, according to EIA, 2012: p.10).

4. These LOCs have catalysed export of various projects in diverse sectors such as agriculture, transportation, communication, manufacturing, energy generation and transmission and rural electrification. Increasingly, Lines of

Credit are being extended for financing Indian project exports, which create in the recipient countries a greater visibility for Indian expertise and project execution capabilities with downstream linkages (Exim Bank of India, 2007: p. 8).

3

Co-operation in the Health Segment, Medical and Pharmaceutical Sectors

This chapter focusses on Nigeria's need for global intervention in health sector in general and Indian assistance in particular. Further, it highlights the bilateral co-operation between India and Nigeria in the health segment and focusses on medical tourism, and the presence of Indian pharmaceutical companies; both public and private, in the West African state. It also deals with the issue of the fake drugs controversy that lead to severe problems for patients in Nigeria and ways in which the two countries have worked together to resolve the issues.

Overview of the Health Scenario in Nigeria

The Nigerian Health Sector

The health sector indices of Nigeria are a cause of concern. There are various death mortalities which are caused due to Human Immunodeficiency Virus/Acquired Immunodeficiency Syndrome (HIV/AIDS), diarrhea and other major communicable diseases such as measles, malaria and pneumonia; conditions arising in the prenatal and deaths caused by other diseases and by injury (WHO 2012: pp. 74-75).

According to the WHO data on Nigeria for the year 2011 "estimates for key MDG-related indicators, including maternal mortality, and mortality and morbidity caused by HIV/AIDS, malaria and tuberculosis per population of 100,000 are 132, 131 and 17 for Tuberculosis among HIV negative people, respectively. Deaths are also caused by cancer, cardiovascular disease and diabetes, and chronic respiratory conditions". These indicators were of concern and an obstacle towards the achievement of the Millennium Development Goal Target 6 (MDG 6)" (WHO, 2013: p. 72).

Life expectancy upto birth is between 48 to 55 years, for men and women respectively, the rate of maternal mortality is upto 545 per 100,000 births, while infant mortality is at 75 per 1,000 births, the basic death rate is 14 deaths per 1,000; 23 per cent of children under five are underweight for their age; 41 per cent of children are immunised against measles and the HIV prevalence rate is now approximately 4.1 per cent (*Ibid*: pp. 74-75).

To deal with the abysmal health indicators the Nigerian government has designed a long term strategy and a vision document discussed below:

Nigeria's New Vision: Health

In Nigeria's Vision 20:2020 document for the health sector, there are a number of challenges. These are: weak systems of governance at the Local Government Areas (LGA) level where the responsibility for Primary Health Care (PHC) services lies. There is limited and uneven access to healthcare services across the country. While the resources for the health sector and per capita health expenditure are low. The Vision document spells out the following objectives to overcome the shortcoming in the health sector.

Objectives for the Health Sector stated in the document are:

1. Creation and sustaining an enabling environment for the delivery of quality healthcare and development in Nigeria;

2. Revitalising integrated service delivery towards a quality, equitable and sustainable healthcare; and

3. Planning and implementing strategies to address the human resources for health needs in order to ensure its availability as well as ensure equity and quality of health care.

The Strategy Envisioned for the Health Sector Includes;

1. Health Service Delivery;

2. Human Resources for Health;

3. Financing for Health;

4. National Health Management Information System;

5. Partnerships for Health;

6. Community Participation and Ownership; and

7. Research for Health.

The Targets for the Health Sector are;

1. Reduce under-five mortality rate from 157 per 1000 in 2008 to 103/1000 live births by 2013;

2. Reduce infant mortality rate from 75/1000 live births in 2008 to 45/1000 live births by 2013;

3. Increase the proportion of one year old immuniszed against measles from 41.4 per cent in 2008 to 80 per cent by 2013;

4. Reduce the maternal mortality ratio from the estimated 545 / 1000 live births in 2008 to 273 / 1000 live births by 2013;

5. Reduce the HIV prevalence among population aged 15-24 years from 19.4 per cent in 2008 to 10 per cent by 2013;

6. Reduce proportion of tuberculosis cases detected and cured under directly observed treatment short course to one per cent by 2013;

7. Increase the proportion of 12-23 months-old children fully immunised from 22.7 per cent in 2008 to 71 per cent by 2013; and

8. Increase the proportion of children under five with fever who are treated with appropriate anti-malarial drugs from 33.3 per cent in 2008 to 65 per cent by 2013 (Nigeria Vision 20:2020, 2010, pp: 160-164).

Nigeria and International Interventions in Health-care

Nigeria's healthcare sector is underdeveloped and the country needs to work with other well-organised agencies that are working in the health sector, import drugs from them and use their facilities for diagnostic and treatment. For instance, the country works closely with the several United Nations (UN) system namely; United Nations Development Programme (UNDP) and United Nations Programme on HIV/AIDS (UNAIDS) as well as the World Health Organisation (WHO).[1]

While the country develops its national capacity in the healthcare sector it is importing quality drugs from countries in the South such as India and China to meet the shortfalls until it has improved its domestic capacity. Several patients get medical visas to travel for treatment in hospitals in India (WHO, 2009).

India and Nigeria: Areas of Convergence in the Health Sector

Nigerians traveling across their state borders for medical treatment; their visit to different countries for medical purpose is termed in popular parlance as "medical tourism". Of the several destinations for Nigerian medical tourists, India is a prominent destination for Nigerians. Nigerian medical tourist can avail medical facilities at metro cities of India such as New Delhi, Mumbai, Chennai, and Hyderabad and in smaller cities of Gurgaon and Kottayam (Placid Way, 2012).

Given the poor government infrastructure and capacity in healthcare sector Nigeria has attempted to improve this sector through international collaboration with countries like India. Because of above reasons Nigerians actively travel to India for medical reason. The common interest of India and Nigeria in the health sector is mutually beneficial in nature. There is a common interest in the sharing and transfer of medical technology to local hospitals in Nigeria, promoting medical tourism of Nigerians to India, sale of good quality and affordable generic Indian drugs and medical equipment to Nigeria (*Ibid*).

Nigeria benefits through trade in pharmaceuticals with India and the transfer of medical technology to Nigeria. The inflow of Nigerian patient's to Indian hospitals provides a market for Indian health sector services to patients from Nigeria as well as including patients abroad.

The India–Africa Forum Summits (IAFS) of 2008 and 2011 have facilitated closer cooperation between India and Nigeria in the healthcare segment, amongst others the areas of cooperation and rationale for the same have been outlined in the IAFS documents and are mentioned below:

India Africa Forum Summits

In 2008 and 2011 Africa and India acknowledge that upgrading and streamlining healthcare systems and increasing access to healthcare for the people of Africa and India is a critical issue and agree to increase cooperation in the field of health promotion and healthcare systems through the following areas of co-operation:

1. India launched the C.V. Raman Fellowship for African researchers in 2008 India Africa sharing experiences, information and expertise on traditional systems of medicine within recognised intellectual property regime;

2. Training and capacity building for health professionals and physicians;

3. Sharing experience and information on healthcare systems development and community health programmes;

4. Linking the centres of excellence in the health sector, such as research and training institutes, etc.;

5. Focus on co-operation in devising and implementing programmes for enhancing universal access to adequate medical services, including developing the tele-medicine infrastructure and technology to enable patients to receive quality health services, such as medical diagnostic and other services to which they would not ordinarily have access due to distance and/or limitation in the availability of specialists;

6. Strengthen the indigenous manufacturing capacities and to make available affordable and quality pharmaceutical products, especially essential medicines. This may also include exchange of technical experts and collaborative efforts;

7. Enhance co-operation in controlling HIV/AIDS, TB, Malaria and other communicable diseases;

8. Co-operation in combating the proliferation and dumping of counterfeit medicines;

9. Local production of oral rehydration therapy (IAFS, 2008);

10. In 2011 India will organise an India-Africa workshop on traditional medicine to highlight the commonalities in approach and sharing of experience;

11. Both sides will strengthen public and private sectors collaboration in the areas of pharmaceutical production and procurement in Africa and India in the framework of pharmaceutical manufacturing plan for Africa;

12. Both sides will support collaboration in research and development in traditional medicine and practices in Africa and India;

13. Both sides agree to share experiences, specialised expertise and best practices in healthcare systems development and community health programmes; and

14. India will collaborate with Africa in training and continuing education for health professionals; the Pan-African e-Network, Tele-Medicine component supports continuing Medical Education (CME) and the training of health professionals in various sectors already part of ongoing bilateral and regional programmes (IAFS, 2011).

It provides for collaborative research in the field of science and technology between countries in Africa and India. Details of the C.V. Raman Fellowship of Government of India for R&D are as follows:

1. It is given to African researchers to work in Indian R and D labs and academic institutions;

2. It was agreed to add a new component of research internship programme under the C.V. Raman Fellowship programme for African students pursuing Master's and Ph.D. degree in science and technology to undertake internship in Indian R&D labs and academic institutions; and

3. To promote capacity building, foster contacts and networking between Indian and African researchers, it was agreed to launch a reciprocal visitation programme under which Indian scientists and faculty members can visit institutions in each other's country up to three weeks duration to deliver pedagogical courses and deliver lectures.

The Department of Science and Technology in consultation with Administrative Uniformity Committee (AUC) will develop annual training calendar (PIB, G.O.I., 2012). During 2010, the C.V. Raman Fellowships were given to five recipients from Nigeria. Out of these three were invited for studying and doing research in India in the fields of endocrinology, cancer research and biotechnology (Modi, 2013: pp. 44). The cooperation has continued over the past years and detailed below:

Nigeria: List of Provisionally Selected Candidates - 2011-12

India will collaborate with Africa in training and continuing education for health professionals. One of the novel initiatives of co-operation is through the

Table 3.1: Post-doctoral Fellowship

No.	*Name of Candidates*	*Parent Institute*	*Host Institute*
1.	Dr Abidemi James Akindele	Department of Pharmacology, University of Lagos	Cancer Pharmacology Division, Indian Institute of Intergrative Medicine (CSIR), Jammu
2.	Dr Edwin Ogechukwu Omeje	Department of Pharmaceutical Chemistry, Department of Pharmaceutical Sciences, University of Nigeria, Nsukka	Department of Endocrinology, Central Drug Research Institute, Lucknow

Source: Department of Science and Technology, Government of India 2011.

Table 3.2: Visiting Fellowship

No.	*Name of Candidates*	*Parent Institute*	*Host Institute*
1.	Dr Ikemefuna Chijioke Uzochukwu	Faculty of Pharmaceutical Sciences, Nnamdi Azikiwe University, Anambra	International Center for Genetic Engineering and Biotechnology, Structural and Computational Biology, New Delhi
2.	Dr Christianah Abimbola Elusiyan	Drug Research and Production Unit, Faculty of Pharmacy, Obafemi Awolowo University, Ile-Ife University	Jaypee University of Information Technology, Solan
3.	Dr Petra Obioma Nnamani	Department of Pharmaceutics, University of Nigeria, Nsukka	Department of Physics, Shivaji University, Kolhapur

Source: Department of Science and Technology, Government of India 2011

Table 3.3: Senior Fellowship

No.	*Name of Candidates*	*Parent Institute*	*Host Institute*
1.	Dr Emmanuel Chinedum Ibezim	Dept. of Pharmaceutics, University of Nigeria, Nsukka	CSIR, Pharmaceutics Division, Lucknow
2.	Dr Anthony Amechi Attama	Department of Pharmaceutics, University of Nigeria, Nsukka	Centre for Nano Science and Nanotechnology, Mahatma Gandhi University, Kottayam
3.	Dr Oluwatoyin Adepeju Odeku	Department of Pharmaceutics and Industrial Pharmacy, Faculty of Pharmacy, University of Ibadan	Department of Pharmaceutics, JSS University, Ooty

Source: Department of Science and Technology, Government of India 2011.

Pan-African e-Network. Its tele-medicine component supports CME and the training of health professionals in various sectors already part of ongoing bilateral and regional programmes.

Pan-African e-Network: India Africa Tele-Medicine

The Pan African e-Network Project was initiated by the visionary former President of India Dr A.P.J. Abdul Kalam. India has created a fibre-optic network to provide satellite connectivity, telemedicine to countries of Africa. Around 48 African countries participated in the project and signed the agreement with Telecommunications Consultants India Ltd. (TCIL) for their participation. This project was carried out in 47 countries out of 48 who actively participated in this project (MEA, 2013).

The Pan-African e-Network Project is a joint collaboration between the Indian government and the African Union, which is the biggest project for distance education and tele-medicine ever undertaken in Africa. This is a remarkable opportunity to provide affordable healthcare and training. It also provides an interface between specialist doctors in the treatment and diagnosis of patients. With this project, India is offering Africa access to some of its best universities and hospitals (New African Magazine, 2012a).

Under this project telemedicine is being provided and awareness is being created through tele-education. Centres have been set up and termed as telemedicine centre in four regional super specialty hospitals in Africa, namely: Republic of Congo, Egypt, Mauritius and Nigeria. The fifth telemedicine centre is in process of being set up in Senegal. In these four telemedicine centres, around 460 telemedicine consultations were setup. CME sessions were started since April 22, 2009 on regular basis in these four regional super specialty hospitals. India provides 2439 CME session in English and 167 CME sessions in French, these sessions were held in these four Indian super specialty hospitals since April 2009 to September 2012 (MEA, 2013).

Under the telemedicine component, patient end locations have already been set up in the 12 Indian Super Specialty Hospitals, namely, The All India Institute of Medical Sciences (AIIMS), New Delhi; Amrita Institute of Medical Sciences, Kochi; Apollo Hospitals, Chennai; CARE Hospital, Hyderabad; Escorts Heart Institute and Research Centre, New Delhi; Fortis Hospital, Noida; Narayana Hrudayalya, Bangalore; Sri Ramchandra Medical Centre, Chennai; Moolchand Hospital, New Delhi; HCG, Bangalore; Dr. Bala Bhai Nanavati Hospital, Mumbai; Sanjay Gandhi Institute of Medical Sciences, Lucknow. These 12 Indian Super Specialty Hospitals have been connected to 48 patient end locations and hospitals in African countries. As per the agreement signed the Government of India (GoI) will continue with its efforts to provide these facilities under the Pan-African e-Network (*Ibid*).

However, though a novel initiative, the Pan Africa e-Network is not a substitute for good healthcare in countries of Africa. There is an urgent need for good medical diagnostics and treatment in countries of Africa as well as the need to produce quality and affordable medicines on the continent, which are at present being supplied by the Indian pharmaceutical sector *(Ibid)*.

India and Nigeria is co-operating in the health sector through medical tourism of Africans to India. Further, Nigeria has an active engagement with countries like India in the health sectors. As there is a convergence of interest between India and Nigeria in setting up Indian hospitals and transferring technology to local hospitals in Nigeria as well as in the sale of quality and affordable Indian generic drugs to Nigeria (*Ibid*).

Through the Abuja declaration, Nigeria pledged to increase government funding for health to at least 15 per cent and urged donor countries to scale up support (WHO, 2011).

The Abuja Declaration of 2001

The meeting of the AU on the Abuja declaration was held in 2001 at Abuja, Nigeria. All the AU members promised that they will allocate at least the 15 per cent of their annual national budget towards improvement of the health sector. In 2001, only two African countries have reached that Abuja target. The two countries— Rwanda and South Africa have achieved the Abuja declaration target of "at least 15 per cent" (*Ibid*: p. 2).

Countries committed to the Abuja declaration have increased the proportion of total government expenditures allocated to health General Government Health Expenditure/General Government Expenditure (GGHE/GGE). The 27 countries that have increased the proportion of total government expenditures allocated to health are namely; Angola, Botswana, Burkina Faso, Burundi, Cameroon, Chad, Comoros, Congo, Côte d'Ivoire, Djibouti, Eritrea, Ghana, Gabon, Guinea Bissau, Lesotho, Liberia, Seychelles, Mali, Mozambique, Nigeria, Rwanda, South Africa, Sao Tome and Principe, Swaziland, Senegal, Uganda and Zambia. Meanwhile, seven countries reduced their relative contributions of government expenditures to health during the period. These are: Benin, Central African Republic, Gambia, Guinea, Malawi, Mauritania and Togo. For other twelve countries; Algeria, Congo, Cape Verde, Democratic Republic Congo, Ethiopia, Egypt, Kenya, Madagascar, Mauritius, Namibia, Niger, Tanzania and Tunisia, there is no obvious trend upwards or downwards (*Ibid* : p. 2).

Despite tremendous progress in the fight against AIDS, TB, Malaria, reproductive health, maternal and child mortality, and human resources for health, most AU countries are not on track to achieve the health MDGs. Part of the explanation is the lack of financial resources, as many nations are challenged to raise adequate funds to provide quality services that deliver results. This was a problem, the main problem that the Abuja declaration was supposed to address (Demmisse, 2013).

The Abuja Declarations and subsequent commitments stimulated sharp increase in resource mobilisation and the scale up of programmes to fight diseases in Africa. During 2006, additional momentum was provided by the emerging international consensus on universal access as a means to attain Millennium Development Goal 6 and other health-related MDGs (Africa Union, 2010: p. 3).

It is notable that the Abuja targets of 15 per cent expenditure on healthcare are unfulfilled despite an overall increase in Development Assistance to Health (DHA) through donor assistance, due to fungibility of the money received, i.e., the money are diverted to other budget heads by the national government (Modi, 2012: p. 33).

The Table 3.4 shows that, the total expenditure on healthcare as percentage of GDP in 2013 for countries of the African continent. From the table it can be seen that the percentage of government expenditure on health for the countries listed are as follows: Burundi (8.1 per cent), Ethiopia (13.7 per cent), Ghana (12.1 per cent), Kenya (5.9 per cent), Liberia (11.1 per cent), Malawi (18.5 per cent), Nigeria (5.07 per cent), Rwanda (23.3 per cent),

Table 3.4: Health Expenditure as Percentage of GDP

Member State	*Total Expenditure on Health as Percentage of Gross Domestic Product*		*General Government Expenditure on Health as Percentage of Total Government Expenditure*		*External Resources for Health as Percentage of Total Expenditure on Health*		*Social Security Expenditure on Health as Percentage of General Government Expenditure on Health*		*Out-of-Pocket Expenditure as Percentage of Private Expenditure on Health*		*Per Capita Government Expenditure on Health (PPP int. $)*	
	2000	2010	2000	2010	2000	2010	2000	2010	2000	2010	2000	2010
Algeria	3.5	4.3	8.8	9.0	0.1	0	35.5	30.0	96.7	94.7	138	291
Angola	2.9	3.4	2.9	6.3	3.0	2.3	0	0	62.8	70.6	37	118
Benin	1.9	4.3	10.0	10.5	38.5	32.8	0.5	0.4	...	91.2	23	36
Botswana	4.7	5.1	7.3	8.7	0.5	8.0	...	...	36.7	12.7	249	459
Burkina Faso	5.1	7.4	8.8	15.7	13.9	36.1	0.8	0.4	94.3	73.8	15	51
Burundi	6.2	9.1	7.5	8.1	19.1	40.9	25.1	23.0	73.0	64.6	7	19
Cameroon	4.4	5.1	5.5	8.5	4.3	7.0	4.2	2.6	94.4	94.5	14	36
Cape Verde	4.8	2.3	9.9	2.5	13.0	19.5	34.9	87.3	95.2	93.7	68	39
Central African Republic	2.2	3.8	12.9	10.4	35.4	25.3	...	...	...	90.3	14	15

(Contd.)

(Contd.Table 3.4)

Member State	*Total Expenditure on Health as Percentage of Gross Domestic Product*		*General Government Expenditure on Health as Percentage of Total Government Expenditure*		*External Resources for Health as Percentage of Total Expenditure on Health*		*Social Security Expenditure on Health as Percentage of General Government Expenditure on Health*		*Out-of-Pocket Expenditure as Percentage of Private Expenditure on Health*		*Per Capita Government Expenditure on Health (PPP int. $)*	
	2000	*2010*	*2000*	*2010*	*2000*	*2010*	*2000*	*2010*	*2000*	*2010*	*2000*	*2010*
Chad	6.3	4.0	13.1	3.3	24.9	7.9	...	...	96.2	96.7	18	15
Comoros	3.6	5.3	9.3	13.1	20.5	15.3	0	0	100	100	14	33
Congo	2.1	2.3	4.8	6.5	4.6	4.6	0	0	98.9	94.2	34	59
Democratic Republic of Congo	4.7	7.5	1.8	10.0	2.8	33.0	...	...	77.3	65.0	<1	7
Cost d'Ivoire	1.4	6.2	7.2	6.8	19.4	8.3	...	...	...	91.1	21	28
Djibouti	4.0	7.9	12.0	14.1	47.7	22.1	11.3	9.6	...	99.1	61	126
Egypt	1.7	4.7	5.6	6.1	3.3	0.6	...	21.0	...	97.7	61	115
Ethiopia	4.3	4.8	8.9	13.7	16.5	36.1	0	0	79.2	80.1	11	26

(Contd.)

(Contd.Table 3.4)

Member State	*Total Expenditure on Health as Percentage of Gross Domestic Product*		*General Government Expenditure on Health as Percentage of Total Government Expenditure*		*External Resources for Health as Percentage of Total Expenditure on Health*		*Social Security Expenditure on Health as Percentage of General Government Expenditure on Health*		*Out-of-Pocket Expenditure as Percentage of Private Expenditure on Health*		*Per Capita Government Expenditure on Health (PPP int. $)*	
	2000	*2010*	*2000*	*2010*	*2000*	*2010*	*2000*	*2010*	*2000*	*2010*	*2000*	*2010*
Equatorial Guinea	1.9	4.2	7.8	7.0	8.8	2.1	0	0	90.9	95.3	69	801
Eritrea	4.5	2.9	2.6	3.6	29.8	35.0	0	0	100	100	9	8
Gabon	2.5	3.5	4.8	6.6	2.6	2.3	5.7	24.9	100	100	123	275
Gambia	3.6	4.4	10.4	11.3	19.1	39.2	0	0	53.7	48.4	17	50
Ghana	4.7	5.2	8.3	12.1	14.5	16.5	0	25.2	64.4	66.7	22	50
Guinea	5.7	6.2	6.4	6.8	13.4	26.7	1.1	4.5	99.5	92.7	6	22
Guinea-Bissau	4.9	7.0	2.3	11.1	30.0	28.5	5.4	1.1	54.7	57.2	10	27
Kenya	4.7	4.4	10.5	5.9	8.0	37.9	10.9	13. 0	80.4	76.6	25	29

(Contd.)

(Contd.Table 3.4)

Member State	*Total Expenditure on Health as Percentage of Gross Domestic Product*		*General Government Expenditure on Health as Percentage of Total Government Expenditure*		*External Resources for Health as Percentage of Total Expenditure on Health*		*Social Security Expenditure on Health as Percentage of General Government Expenditure on Health*		*Out-of-Pocket Expenditure as Percentage of Private Expenditure on Health*		*Per Capita Government Expenditure on Health (PPP int. $)*	
	2000	*2010*	*2000*	*2010*	*2000*	*2010*	*2000*	*2010*	*2000*	*2010*	*2000*	*2010*
Lesotho	7.0	11.5	6.3	13.8	3.1	18.2	0	0	74.0	69.0	35	129
Liberia	5.9	16.4	6.7	11.1	9.2	42.4	0	0	50.3	25.8	4	17
Libya	1.9	3.0	6.0	4.0	0	0.7	...	...	...	100	214	401
Madagascar	3.7	3.6	15.5	13.5	20.1	9.5	...	...	52.8	68.3	20	20
Malawi	3.0	8.4	9.0	18.5	53.4	58.1	0	0	...	53.3	16	55
Mali	6.0	6.5	7.5	12.3	8.2	22.2	1.8	0.7	99.1	99.6	13	30
Mauritania	6.0	6.1	12.9	13.1	11.2	7.4	8.7	8.5	94.5	94.5	48	91
Mauritius	3.7	6.2	8.7	10.8	1.4	1.9	...	...	74.6	88.8	159	365
Morocco	4.1	5.4	3.8	5.4	0.5	0.8	0	...	76.6	88.3	31	77
Namibia	6.1	5.5	6.9	6.5	3.8	25.5	1.8	2.7	18.2	17.9	168	209

(Contd.)

(Contd. Table 3.4)

Member State	*Total Expenditure on Health as Percentage of Gross Domestic Product*		*General Government Expenditure on Health as Percentage of Total Government Expenditure*		*External Resources for Health as Percentage of Total Expenditure on Health*		*Social Security Expenditure on Health as Percentage of General Government Expenditure on Health*		*Out-of-Pocket Expenditure as Percentage of Private Expenditure on Health*		*Per Capita Government Expenditure on Health (PPP int. $)*	
	2000	*2010*	*2000*	*2010*	*2000*	*2010*	*2000*	*2010*	*2000*	*2010*	*2000*	*2010*
Mozambique	6.2	6.3	17.0	10.4	25.3	62.2	0.3	20.3	40.6	25.0	19	30
Nigeria	4.6	5.4	4.2	5.7	16.2	8.7	0	0	92.7	95.6	20	40
Niger	3.4	4.8	8.4	11.1	40.4	32.7	3.3	1.3	80.6	84.0	7	18
Rwanda	4.2	10.4	8.2	23.3	52.0	48.0	6.4	9.2	40.7	49.4	10	66
Sao Tome and Principe	8.4	7.5	9.0	5.6	34.8	20.3	0	0	76.1	87.8	124	53
Senegal	4.3	5.8	8.5	12.1	17.4	18.4	8.8	3.9	91.6	78.5	22	63
Sierra Leone	17.5	20.8	14.2	11.7	5.5	26.8	0	0	94.9	91.4	15	26
Seychelles	4.8	3.3	7.3	9.3	4.3	4.2	5.0	1.1	99.0	68.2	690	741
Somalia	2.4	...	4.2	...	40.1	...	0	...	100	...	8	...

(Contd.)

(Contd.Table 3.4)

Member State	*Total Expenditure on Health as Percentage of Gross Domestic Product*		*General Government Expenditure on Health as Percentage of Total Government Expenditure*		*External Resources for Health as Percentage of Total Expenditure on Health*		*Social Security Expenditure on Health as Percentage of General Government Expenditure on Health*		*Out-of-Pocket Expenditure as Percentage of Private Expenditure on Health*		*Per Capita Government Expenditure on Health (PPP int. $)*	
	2000	*2010*	*2000*	*2010*	*2000*	*2010*	*2000*	*2010*	*2000*	*2010*	*2000*	*2010*
South Africa	8.1	8.7	10.9	12.4	0.3	2.2	3.3	2.9	23.1	13.9	...	...
South Sudan	...	2.1	...	4.0	...	21.4	...	...	...	96.4	...	...
Sudan	3.3	7.2	7.6	10.3	4.5	2.9	...	11.1	91.6	96.1	10	45
Swaziland	5.3	7.8	10.5	13.7	5.8	14.4	0	0	42.4	42.3	111	292
Tanzania	3.4	7.2	10.2	11.1	27.8	39.6	0	4.5	83.5	52.4	11	39
Togo	5.3	7.5	8.5	15.4	5.9	18.2	11.7	6.5	88.2	84.6	12	34
Tunisia	5.4	5.7	8.1	10.8	0.9	0.3	28.9	47.7	80.1	87.8	161	295
Uganda	6.6	9.2	7.3	10.8	28.3	27.6	0	0	56.7	64.8	12	27
Zambia	5.7	6.0	9.4	16.0	17.8	43.7	0	0	80.4	66.7	27	56
Zimbabwe	...	...	...	...	...	...	...	...	...	...	...	...

Source: WHO 2013: pp. 132-139

Sierra Leone (11.07 per cent), South Africa (12.4 per cent) and Uganda (10.8 per cent). These countries expend a higher percentage on health as compared to several other countries of the continent (WHO, 2013).

In 2013, according to the WHO statistics four countries spend less than five per cent of their GDP on the health sector. These countries are: Cape Verde (2.5 per cent), Chad (3.3 per cent), Libya (4.0 per cent) and South Sudan (4.0 per cent) (*Ibid*).

In 2000 and 2010 the general expenditure on health as a percentage of total government expenditure GDP for Nigeria was 4.2 per cent and 5.7 per cent, respectively. According to Abuja declaration every country should spend 15 per cent of their GDP on health but Nigeria spends only about 5.7 per cent because the healthcare sector has not been of priority for the government (*Ibid*).

A large number of countries; Benin, Burkina Faso,Central African Republic, Democratic Republic of Congo, Djibouti, Eritrea, Gambia, Ghana, Madagascar, Malawi, Mozambique, Namibia, Niger, Rwanda, Sao Tome and Principe, Sierra Leone, Uganda, United Republic of Tanzania and Zambia receive over 20 per cent of their funds for their health sector through donor funding (Modi, 2011: p.124).

There is a negative impact on domestic government spending on health for every US dollar of DAH to government, due to fungibility of donor assistance that is the substitution for the help of domestic government spending (*Ibid*: p. 33).

Special African Health Summit *(Abuja+12 Summit)*

Nigeria announced a special summit of the African Union heads of State and Government, tagged Abuja+12, to develop modules to augment and attempt implementing programmes of the Action Committee of AIDS Watch Africa (AWA 10-15, July 2013). The meeting was chaired by the Ethiopian Prime Minister, Haile-Mariam Desalegn.

In a communiqué issued the heads of State, the members renewed their commitment to intensify their efforts towards the realisation of the objectives of AWA. According to the communiqué, "AU member states (aimed) to develop a sustainable investment plan for health, particularly AIDS, TB and Malaria, with year-on-year increase in domestic funding. AWA will play a key and leadership role in the forthcoming special Summit of the AU Heads of Government (Abuja+12 Summit) in July in Abuja, Nigeria" (SAFPI, 2013).

Thus, the governments in Africa are concerned about dealing with communicable and non-communicable diseases and aware of the fact that expenditure on the health sector needs to be stepped up. However, in the meantime because the domestic health sector in several countries in Africa is not up to the mark patients from across the continent seek treatment in countries abroad (*Ibid*).

While Nigeria attempts to overhaul its healthcare sector and upgrade its hospitals Indian hospitals cater to Nigerian patients who travel to India for treatment.

Concept of Medical Tourism and Nigerian Patients in India

Nigerians come for treatment to India and other destinations in the world. The following section of this chapter deals with:

1. Concept of medical tourism and Nigerian patients in India.

2. Indian expertise in setting up hospitals in Nigeria: a case study of the Primus hospital, at Abuja.

3. The export of Indian medicines and generics to Africa by reputed pharmaceutical companies.

Medical tourism can be broadly defined as "moving of people from their home countries to destination countries to receive medical, dental, and surgical as well as other multiple medical facilities. Generally medical tourism is practiced by people who can afford (treatment) financially and can get better access to healthcare in destination countries than their home country" (Medical Tourism Association, 2012).

Medical tourists come to India especially from Ghana, Kenya, Nigeria, Tanzania and the rest of Africa. A new trend in medical tourism to India is predominant. Those patients who are not in critical section or seeking treatment for life threatening diseases like cancer but for general wellness and treatable diseases can also combine vacations to exotic destinations in India with their medical treatment, though this is not generally the case (*Ibid*).

There are several reasons for medical tourism to in India. Medical tourism is boosted by the involvement of the Indian corporate sector, the Indian tourism industry and private and public Indian hospitals (Hospital of India, 2012).

Local Nigerians are attracted towards Indian because as compared to industrialised nations that offer costly healthcare, India is comparatively affordable and favourable in terms of currency exchange rates and state of the art medical technology (*Ibid*).

Besides, India provides relatively high quality medical services at relatively lower costs and therefore it has become a hot spot for medical tourism. The Indian medical tourism industry comprises of around $ 2 billion and attracts medical tourists approximately 150,000 medical tourism per year from all over the world (New African Magazine, 2012a). There are several private sector hospitals in India that are the main hubs and attract medical tourists from across the world including in Africa.

Substandard medical facilities in Nigeria compel patients to avoid seeking treatment in their own country. However, for long-term ailment procedures which require continuous supervision and frequent visits to hospitals, travelling to other countries like India would not be easy or preferred by patients (Modi, 2013 pp. 45).

In India, Nigerian patients and other medical tourist from different parts of world to avail and take advantage of vision care, cosmetic surgery, wellness programmes, and surgeries in orthopaedic, cardiac and musculoskeletal disorders. Medical facilities for diseases like chronic ailments, cancer, alternative medicines and general medicines, vision or Laser-Assisted in Situ Keratomileusis (LASIK) care and dental care are provided and serve as a major source of attraction for medical tourists from abroad (Placid Way, 2012).

The Chain of Apollo Hospitals

For medical services Nigerians go to hospital for ailments that include Cardiology and Cardiothoracic Surgery, Orthopedic and Joint Replacement Surgery, Spine Surgery, Oncology, Medical and Surgical Gastroenterology, Neurology and Neurosurgery, Nephrology and Urology, Critical Care Medicine, Cyber Knife Robotic Radio Surgery, Birmingham Hip Replacement Surgery, Cosmetic Surgery, Bariatric Surgery, Liver Transplants, Infertility Management, Hand and Micro Surgery and Bone Marrow Transplants (*Ibid*).

Several Apollo Hospitals[2] in India were the first in the country to receive international healthcare accreditation, being approved by the prestigious US-based Joint Commission International (JCI) (*Ibid*).[6]

The Popular Treatments sought in India by Nigerian Medical Tourists are for;

1. Alternative medicine;
2. Bone-marrow transplant;
3. Cardiac bypass surgery;
4. Eye surgery; and
5. Orthopaedic surgery (Akinboade, 2012).

Medical tourism is facilitated by medical visas given in several countries abroad to make it easy for patients to come to India for treatment.

Medical Visas

The Government of India has introduced 'medical visa' for foreigners who come to India for medical treatment usually for extended periods. The "medical visa" is admissible to all foreigners seeking medicare in recognised specialty hospitals or treatment centres. The initial period of such a visa is for a year or for the period of treatment, whichever is less.

This arrangement too many Nigerians is less cumbersome as compared to the stress they will go through for getting visas to countries like US, UK or even Switzerland (*Ibid*). The ties between Nigeria and India are vibrant and growing. During 2012 almost 40,000 Nigerians obtained Indian, (includes visas for medical and business tourism) (MEA 2013: p. 3).

Visas Details

The Indian High Commission reserves the right of deciding the duration of visa irrespective of the fees tendered at the time of making application. Visas can be applied for in person at the High Commission of India in Lagos (India Abuja 2005). Citizens of Economic of West African States (ECOWAS) do not require entry permits into Nigeria. All visitors not exempted from entry permits are advised to apply and obtain appropriate visas from the nearest Nigerian Mission Embassy, High Commission or consulate before entry into Nigeria as visas cannot be issued at the port of entry (Nigeria HC 2013).

Case Study of Nigerian Patients in India

Nigerian patients have been successfully treated at Indian hospitals because of accuracy in diagnosis of patients at Indian hospitals. There are several cases that can be given as examples of this. Among them three fascinating case studies are discussed below which reflects on the good quality of medical facilities especially in private Indian hospitals. These cases are as follows:

1. The first case is of an 18 month infant from Nigeria, Dike Ezeanya who received successful swap of liver transplant at Sir Ganga Ram hospital in New Delhi (Zee News 2009).

2. The second case is of the 'metallic lady' named Margaret Eremionkhale who suffered from Rheumatoid Arthritis (RA), joint pains since 2003. She is now surviving on metallic hips, metallic knees and a metallic spine. The entire treatment cost her around Rs. 22 lakh ($47,800) (India Africa Connect 2013a).

3. The third case is of 51 years old Morufu Shuaibu was also successfully treated in India. A bullet was embedded in his body since a decade, as she was a victim of riot in Nigeria, was removed in India (Sonkar: Aalatimes 2011).

All these success stories have helped in the publicity of Indian hospitals not only through the media but also by word of mouth by patients who received best facilities and medical treatment in India.

Nigeria is collaborating with India in the health sector to increase its healthcare capabilities and build physical infrastructure such as multi specialty hospitals and trained medical persons with the help of Indian expertise. To provide treatment closer to home, Indian hospitals have partnered with the local set up as in the case of the Primus Hospital at Abuja, Nigeria.

Indian high tech hospitals have sealed a deal to set up collaborative medical services in Port Harcourt, Rivers State. The new deal will turn the First Rivers Hospital Limited (FRHL) into a world-class medical tourist centre in Africa.

India's Top High Tech Hospitals in Nigeria

In 2013, the Nigerian hospital signed two different agreements in the city of Pune, (India) with Ruby Hall Clinic and Trans-medical Healthcare Limited. The agreements were facilitated by Reneva International Ltd., a management and training consultancy firm based in Port Harcourt. This agreement, medical cases can be properly examined and successfully managed in Nigeria without the extra burden of overseas travels while only complicated surgeries can be directed to Ruby Hall Clinics for specialist care requirements which of course will minimise the cost of medical care to patients and their families.

Details indicated that "the parties in these agreements agreed to upgrade the facilities and healthcare services at First Rivers Hospital (Port Harcourt) to a world class level with the latest technologies in X-rays, sonography, CT scan/MRI, cathlab, dialysis centre, diagnostic laboratory, video conferencing suite, etc. as well as providing online/real time and direct access to specialist consultants' expertise at Ruby Hall Clinic, Pune, (India)".

Ruby Hall Clinic is indicated as the award-winning hospital for the best medical tourism facility in India in 2012, awarded by the Ministry of Tourism Government of India. It is India's most preferred medical destination with internationally renowned healthcare facility (Business Day, 2013).

Primus Super Specialty Hospital in Abuja

At present the Primus Super Specialty Hospital (popularly known as the Indian hospital) located in Abuja is an example of collaboration between the two countries. It has brought Indian medical skills to the country, which has provided access to a large population who are due to various reasons, not able to travel abroad for treatment. The hospital has been designed and constructed using some of the most advanced medical technology, available in the world. The hospital is a state of the art multi-specialty facility committed to providing care through professional excellence. It will provide high quality and cost effective healthcare services locally to Nigerian patients. It is expected that this concept would be a good start in bringing the world class healthcare to Nigeria (Modi, 2013: p. 45).

Primus International Super Specialty Hospital has set new benchmarks in medical care with prominent surgeons from across the globe, excellent infrastructure and state of art advanced technology. It has capacity of 120 beds, with vision to expand to 250 beds by 2012 (Primus Hospital, 2011).

Healthcare Facilities at Primus Hospital

In Africa where healthcare facilities is still a challenge, Primus decided to provide a Super

Specialised Surgical centre in the capital city of Nigeria located in West Africa (Infinities 2012 pp. 62-63)[37]. Achla Dewan, Chairperson, said "till now the people of Nigeria were going to other parts of the world for the treatments and for even smaller ailments which were adding to their vows along with illness both financially and mentally. Financial burden was too much because of cost incurred in treatment, boarding, lodging and opportunity cost, this in turn also leads to a huge foreign exchange loss by the country. In order to make the medical services better in the country, Primus has opened up this specialised surgical centre to cater to the patients of not only Nigeria but the whole West Africa"[4] (*Ibid*: pp. 62-63).[8]

Medical Care at Primus

Primus has set new benchmarks in the field of medical care in Nigeria. Primus International Specialty Hospital is a world class hospital with state of the art facility successfully conducted the first bariatric surgery in Nigeria (Abuja). Bariatric surgery is a specialise kind of operation carried out on patients who suffer from obesity. Nigeria has recorded a major break-through in its healtcare policy following the establishment of a world class hospital with state of the art facility to carter for patients with life threatening ailment by an Indian Healthcare expert in the Federal Capital Territory (FCT). They brought the best of equipment worth billions of Naira and delivering services to help the people of Nigeria. (*Ibid*)

The hospital has adopted the latest technology and equipment to strengthen the medical processes and procedures to achieve the set objectives and the instruction of regular training programmes for staff. Residents of Abuja with various ailments have continued to throng the newly opened Primus International Super

Speciality Hospital in Karu, Abuja for medicare (Primus Hospital Nigeria, 2012).

Case Studies of Treatment at Primus Hospital

1. Chukwuocha, Lilian Ijeoma, was unable to stand and walk. After the spine surgery on 11th November, 2011, he can now walk and stand without pain.

2. Rev. Fr. Joseph Etim had severe back pain and stiffness in his right shoulder. On 22nd February, 2012 he came for treatment to Primus and his health improved.

3. Nana Fatimah Sulaiman was treated for orthopaedic problems in February 2012, and she recovered very well (*Ibid*).

There are a lot of challenges in the health sector and therefore several stakeholders have to work as a team. The government, private investors and other stake holders must invest in healthcare so that quality and standards can be brought to an acceptable level. It is hoped that Nigerian doctors who are abroad can come back and contribute to the health sector in the country (Ojeme, 2013).

Other Indian hospitals such as Apollo hospital, renowned for attracting patients across the world has planned for expansion in Africa and will own hospitals in Botswana, Nigeria and Tanzania in the years aheads (New African Magazine, 2012a).[9] In addition to medical treatment Indian companies also export quality pharmaceutical products to Nigeria.

Export of Indian Medicine/Generic to Africa by Reputed Pharmaceutical Companies

Indian pharmaceutical companies are the largest producers and supplier of good quality generic drugs globally, African markets that are often very price competitive and therefore affordable Anti Retroviral (ARV) and anti-malaria drugs manufactured in India help African nations and their public health departments to cope up with the treatment of these diseases (New African Magazine, 2012a).

Indian export to Africa includes pharmaceutical goods and equipment, resources and generic drugs which make up around 11.1 per cent of India's total export to Africa. Indian Government and private Indian pharmaceutical companies have ventured successfully in Africa[6] (*Ibid*).[10]

Indian pharmaceuticals companies' heavy footmark in Africa is a notable marker of India-Africa engagement. Africa accounted for 14 per cent of India's $ 8 billion pharmaceutical exports in 2008-09 and the trade has growing. The India Pharma sector was valued at $ 12 billion in early 2012 and is projected to double its global export to $ 25 billion during 2013-14. Though the US and Europe are the leading destinations for India's Pharma products. South Africa is a major importer of Indian drugs, mainly generic ARVs medicines (Modi, 2012: p. 34).

Indian Pharmaceutical Companies in Africa

India now has the third largest pharmaceuticals industry in the world and is the largest supplier in terms of generic drugs. By 2015, the industry is expected to be worth around $ 20 billion. African countries have been increasing their imports from India, and Indian companies, many based in South Africa, are garnering a larger share of the continental market (New African Magazine, 2012 b).

The three Indian firms with the biggest presence in Africa are Ranbaxy, Cipla and Dr Reddy's. Ranbaxy is India's biggest pharmaceutical firm and is truly global, operating in 46 countries with customers in more than 125 countries. Its African subsidiary, set up in 1998, is

South Africa's fifth-largest generic company after the acquisition of pharmaceutical firm Be-Tabs in 2006 (*Ibid*).

According to the 2011 Annual Report of Ranbaxy, "Ranbaxy's upbeat attitude about its future role in Africa is clear. Africa has been a major growth story for Ranbaxy and continues to invest in the region to further expand business." Its sales in Africa grew by 23 per cent in 2011, to $ 189 m while its sales in Nigeria grew 17 per cent to $ 26 m in 2011(*Ibid*).

Dr Reddy's, another large Indian pharmaceuticals firm, has also made impressive progress in Africa. After entering the continent through a subsidiary, Dr Reddy's entered the market directly in 2004. It is now the 18th biggest generic company in South Africa in terms of value. The revenue generation for 2010 has been $ 9.4m, representing more than two fold increase. The firm also launched nine new products, including Valaciclovir and Imipenem+Cilastatin. It has completed the upgrading of its plant in South Africa and has received approval from the Medicines Control Council (MCC) for a manufacturing facility in Roodepoort, South Africa. Cipla Medpro South Africa, the South African subsidiary of the Indian firm Cipla, also recorded a 28 per cent increase in revenue in the six months ended 30th June 2012 to R1, 080 billion ($ 123 m) [7](*Ibid*).[11]

Firms are also looking beyond South Africa and are keen to break into other markets in the region. Ranbaxy, for example, "is eager to strengthen its presence in Nigeria, the second largest market for the pharmaceutical industry in Africa. It recently announced its intention to open a green field manufacturing plant in 2013" (*Ibid*).

Competition with China for Markets in Africa

China's huge vaccine manufacturing capacities are posing a major threat to India's dominance in the global vaccine market according to the Pharmaceuticals Export Promotion Council (Pharmexcil) of India. P.V. Appaji, the director general of Pharmexcil stated, "India would lose its supremacy in the global vaccine market unless the government comes forward to help the domestic vaccine makers. China has come up with much larger capacity units which are a big worry for the entrepreneur driven Indian vaccine sector" (Prohaska, 2012).

Indian Companies Introduce New Drugs to Africa

Some Indian companies have successfully introduced new drugs to the African markets for example, "in the spring of 2012, Ranbaxy introduced a new anti-malarial drug, Synriam. It is claimed to have a 95 per cent cure rate and relieve symptoms of the illness. In September, Cipla's new proposed drug to combat Malaria was approved by the World Health Organisation as well. Indian companies have adopted a number of common strategies to build their business presence in Africa" [8](New African Magazine, 2012b).[12]

Nonetheless, in Nigeria, as in other African countries, local companies have a long way to go before they can compete with the already established foreign firms. In Nigeria, international firms like GlaxoSmithKline and Pfizer still dominate the market. But India is trying to get a larger share of the market through the sale of generics (New African Magazine, 2012c).

Trade in Generic Drugs

India is already big in generic drugs[9] and her generic drug exports totaled to about $ 11 billion in the year 2012.[13] India has a sustained global campaign to capture an estimated $ 40 billion worth of additional market for generic or copied medicines as patents are held by multinationals on sophisticated medicines (Sen: *The Economic Times*, 2012).

Indian generics are affordable and save lives. India has long been considered the pharmacy of the developing world and Indian generics such as ARVs provide medicines at a fraction of the cost of drugs produced by multinationals. Eighty per cent of people living with HIV who receive treatment in developing countries use Indian generic ARVs and over 90 per cent of pediatric AIDS medicines are supplied by Indian generics (Modi, 2013: p. 45). While emphasis is on countries with ageing population such as Japan, which needs more of cheaper medicine, large markets such as Africa and Latin America are also in focus. They are much cheaper than the original patented drugs and their use helps lower treatment costs (Sen: *The Economics Times*, 2012).

India's huge generic drug industry has been a major supplier of vastly cheaper copycat medicines to treat diseases such as Cancer, TB and AIDS for those who cannot afford expensive branded versions across the developing world (Global Post, 2013).

In Nigeria, growth is positive with pharmaceuticals expenditure projected to grow from N143.65 billion ($921 m) in 2011 to N167.28 billion ($ 1.05 billion) in 2012, according to Business Monitor International's (BMI) report that, "the country's healthcare and pharmaceuticals industry for the third quarter of 2012" (New African Magazine, 2012d).

The next section studies how the contribution of Indian pharmaceutical industry for exports can be increased by involving exports globally.

In 2011, India exports in drugs, pharmaceuticals and fine chemicals, USA stands first for all the five years in import of India's produce. The reason of Indian pharmaceutical companies' interest towards USA might be high margins of profits and well understood regulatory procedures. In addition to this, Indian pharmaceutical companies have developed their products to the standards of U S Food and Drug Administration (USFDA or FDA) which are also well accepted and easily approved in all other regulated markets in the world (Rau and Appaji, 2012: p. 46).

Table 3.5: Indian Exports of Drugs, Pharmaceuticals and Fine Chemical to Countries in Africa as Compared to Global Market

Rank	*Country*	*Year : 2011 / in crore*
1.	USA	10856.00
2.	Russia	1907.09
3.	UK	1723.84
4.	Germany	1579.17
5.	South Africa	1464.98
6.	Nigeria	1038.86
7.	Brazil	1008.64
8.	Netherlands	876.01
9.	Canada	860.90
10.	Kenya	842.43
11.	Turkey	728.90
12.	Vietnam	660.70
13.	Israel	633.87
14.	Spain	610.93
15.	Ghana	606.74
16.	China	604.31
17.	France	597.96
18.	Italy	590.58
19.	Sri Lanka	582.33
20.	Ukraine	557.11
	Top 20 Sub Total	28331.36
	World Trade	47363.33
	% Contribution by to 20.	59.82

Source: Rau and Appaji 2012: pp. 45-46.

In 2011 China's imports from India were valued at Rs 604.31 crore. This is a clear indication of China's revolutionary changes of in-house manufactures relating to drugs, pharmaceutical and fine chemical. Brazil, Nigeria and South Africa are markets for Indian pharmaceutical companies in export of drugs, pharmaceutical and fine chemical (*Ibid*: pp. 45-46).

Several plans and policies are undertaken to increase domestic production of drugs and other equipment's in Nigeria to enable the country to achieve its Millennium Development Goals (MDGs). For example, Nigeria put a ban on import of pharmaceutical products which could be produced within the country locally in 2005. But this ban had a negative impact. It resulted in scarcity of essential goods in Nigeria, price hike and most disastrous effect was opening of market of fake drugs manufactures who took advantage of this scarcity of pharmaceutical products. The outcome of this was that around the world Nigeria was one of only eight countries in world with high drug prices in January, 2010. This also resulted in providing way for too many fake drugs in Nigeria. Indian pharmaceutical companies have developed their products to the standards of USFDA which are well accepted and easily approved in all other regulated markets in the world (*Ibid*: pp. 45-46). In such a situation India became a leading supplier of pharmaceutical products to Nigeria and Nigerian consumers gave a good response to drugs produced in India. But still Nigeria faces challenge of fake drugs. Both the countries have to deal with problem by regulatory agencies of two countries under terms of Memorandum of Understanding (MoU) (Modi, 2013: p. 44).

Fake/Counterfeit Drug

Nigeria seized a consignment of fake drugs made in China but carrying the "Made in India" label, an official delegation from the African country and Indian industry here with the assurance that they were more vigilant against counterfeit medicines and open to generic pharmaceuticals (India Africa Connect, 2013b). Director General Paul Ohri Nigeria's National Agency for Food and Drug Administration and Control (NAFDAC) stated that, "It had detected a large consignment of anti-malarial drugs from China, which had been labeled "Made in India", being sold in that country. It snowballed into a diplomatic issue, with the Indian government lodging a strong protest with the Chinese authorities. It was an unfortunate incident, but it has opened up a lot of opportunities in fight against counterfeits, with the Indian government involved as it has interests in the issue. Incidentally, China and India are the top exporters of drugs to Nigeria, where foreign made pharmaceuticals account for 60 per cent of the market. At an interaction with representatives of Indian Pharma companies at the Federation of Indian Chamber of Commerce and Industry (FICCI) made clear that Nigeria did not plan to define counterfeit drugs to include generics. Africa accounts for 15 per cent of India's Pharma exports worth $ 6.32 billion (*Ibid*). The Indian government and manufacturers zealously guard their established name in the pharmaceutical sector. In response to a news report titled "Counterfeit Medicine from Asia threatens lives in Africa" available in the Guardian newspaper on December 24, 2012, the Ministry of External Affairs (Government of India), issued a clarification via press statement to counter the assertion (MEA 2012a).

The MEA Gave Details

No fake medicines have been sent from India to the continent of Africa. Allegations of the nature mentioned in the Guardian, when they have surfaced previously have been investigated both in Africa and in India and have been found to be baseless with the origin of such drugs not being from India. As the Guardian report itself acknowledges, India has stepped up oversight on this subject. The Government of India continues to interact extensively with countries in Africa to provide quality medicines at affordable prices. The Government of India is committed to continue this cooperation in the strong belief that this is an ideal means of enhancing South-South Cooperation and engagement (Ibid).

To curb the problem of 'negative publicity' in several countries, the department of commerce, Government of India, has given advice to Pharmexcil, a body set up by Ministry of Commerce and Industry for promoting the export of pharmaceuticals and healthcare products and service from India. To start a new brand Pharma India campaign globally organised to raise, among other things, consciousness about the Indian Pharma sector, to protect this sector from assertion acquired interests and conform to the international consumers that Indian generics life saves, and is reasonable and of international values (Modi, 2012: p. 35).

Conclusion

In this chapter India and Nigeria's cooperation in the health segment has been analysed. The focus of this chapter is on the cooperation in the medical and pharmaceutical sectors between the two countries. India's major pharmaceuticals companies are investing on a large scale in Nigerian market and their presence in Nigeria is growing. Constraints like fake drugs are affecting the exports of these companies but these issues are being handled by the Governments of India and Nigeria. New trends like medical tourism have emerged as a new area of collaboration where with the help of high end technological equipment in Indian hospitals and skilled medical personnel, Nigerian patients have gained immensely from the Indian healthcare sector. In addition, the partnership between India and Nigeria is mutually beneficial as medical and health sector in

Nigeria as well as in other African countries and Nigeria avail better access to healthcare facilities by using medium of medical tourism in India and by growing presence of India healthcare facilities with Nigeria. Most AU countries are not yet on the track to achieve the health MDGs and part of the explanation can be found in the lack of financial resources available to them. In 2001, the Abuja declaration recognised this as a potential problem ten years ago highlighting the importance for governments in AU countries of giving greater weight to health in the allocation of government revenues, while at the same time urging donor countries to increase their funding levels (WHO, 2011: p. 5).

The growing presence of Indian healthcare facilities within Nigeria and assistance through digital technology such as the Pan-Africa e-Network, it is expected that the healthcare sector of Nigeria will improve. To conclude, in the coming years, Indian and Nigeria will have many opportunities to work together on several areas in the healthcare segment.

References

African Union (2010), 'Five- Year Review of the Abuja call for Accelerated Action Towards Universal', Access to HIV/AIDS, Tuberculosis and Malaria Services by 2010, Progress Report (2006-2010), Special Session of the African Union Conference of Ministers of Health Geneva, Switzerland, MIN/Sp/AU/CAMH4/3, Available at: <http://www.au.int/en/> (Accessed on 15/05/2012).

Akinboade, B. (2012), 'Why Nigerians are Rushing to India for', NFC Media Group, 19 January, Available at: <http://www.nigeriafilms.com/news/15408/54/>(Accessed on 07/02/2013).

Business Day (2013), '*India's top hitech hospitals set up African centre in Port Harcourt*' Business Day Media Ltd. Magazine, Available at <http://businessdayonline.com/2013/07/indias-top-hitech-hospitals-set-up-african-centre-in-port-harcourt/> (Accessed on 23/07/2013).

Cipla Caring for Life (1935), Available at: <http://www.cipla.com/Home/Partnering/Locations.aspx ?mid=1295>(Accessed on 07/12/2012).

Demmisse, E. (2013), '*The 50th Anniversary of the AU: Time to Recommit to the Promises of Abuja*', Huff Post, 22 May, Available at: <http://www.huffingtonpost.com/endalkachew-demmisse/the-50th-anniversary-of-t_b_3317356.html> (Accessed on 22/05/2013).

Department of Science and Technology (2011), 'C. V. Raman International Fellowship for African Researchers', Government of India, New Delhi, Available at: <http://www.dst.gov.in/whats_new/whats_new12/C_V_Raman_Fellowship_AF_R-2011-2012.pdf> (Accessed on 16/02/2013).

Global Post – International News (2013), '*India's Top Court Backs Generics in key Drug Patent Ruling*', Available at: <http://www.globalpost.com/dispatch/news/afp/130401/indias-top-court-backs-generics-key-drug-patent-ruling-1> (Accessed on 07/12/2012).

High Commission of India in Nigeria (2005), 'Visa Services', Available at: <http://www.indianhcabuja.com/Visa-Services.htm> (Accessed on 15/05/2013).

Hospital of India (2012), Available at: <http://www.hospitalsofindia.co.in/EBroucher.pdf> (Accessed on 07/02/2012).

IAFS (2008), '*Plan of Action of the Framework for Co-operation on the India Africa Forum Summit*', Addis Ababa, Embassy of India: First IAFS, April 8-9, New Delhi, Available at: <http://www.indianembassy.gov.et/?q=node/21> (Accessed on 26/02/2013).

IAFS (2011), '*Plan of Action of the Framework for Co-operation on the India Africa Forum Summit*', Addis Ababa, Embassy of India: Second IAFS, 25th May, New Delhi, Available at: <http://www.indianembassy.gov.et/?q=node/21> (Accessed on 26/02/2013).

India Africa Connect (2013a), 'Indian Surgeons Help Nigerian Woman', Indo Asian News Service, Available at: <http://

www.indiaafricaconnect.in/index.php?param=news/3369/africa-in-india/118> (Accessed on 07/12/2012).

India Africa Connect (2013b), 'Nigeria More Vigilant against Fake Drugs', Indo Asian News Service, Available at: http://www.indiaafricaconnect.in/index.php?param=news/191/health-education/106 (Accessed on 04/03/2013).

Infinities (2012), *'Focus on India's Ties with Nigeria Benin, Cameroon' and Chad'*, Edition, 5th Siddis: the African of India, High Commission of India, Abuja, Available at:<http://indianhcabuja.com/docs/InfiniTies_2012_ Magazine. pdf> (Accessed on 27/05/2013).

MEA (2010), 'India's Foreign Relations', Government of India, New Delhi, Available at: <http://www.mea.gov.in/Images/pdf/Indias_Foreign_Relations_2010.pdf> (Accessed on 07/12/2012).

MEA (2012a), *'Response to a Report in the Guardian Newspaper on Counterfeit Medicines in Africa'*, Government of India, New Delhi, Available at: http://www.mea.gov.in/mediabriefings. htm?dtl/21019/Response+to+a+report+in+The+Guardian+ newspaper+on+counterfeit+medicines+in+Africa (Accessed on 30/02/2013).

MEA (2013), *'Pan African e-Network Project'*, Government of India, New Delhi, Available at: http://mea.gov.in/portal/Foreign Relation/Pan_African_e_docx_for_xp.pdf (Accessed on 07/02/2013).

Medical Tourism Association (2013-14), *'Medical Tourism FAQ's'*, Medical Tourism, Available at: <http://www.medical tour ismassociation.com/en/medicaltourism-faq-s.html> (Accessed on 07/02/2013).

Modi, R. (2012), *'Revamping Africa's Healthcare'*, Africa Quarterly, Indian Journal of Africa Affairs, Vol. 52, No. 3, Aug-Oct , Indian Council for Cultural Relations, New Delhi.

Modi, R. (2013) *'Infinities Focus on India's Ties with Nigeria, Benin, and Cameroon* and Chad', 6th Edition 2013, Available at: <http://www.indianhcabuja.com/docs/InfiniTies2013.pdf> (Accessed on 07/02/2013).

Modi, R. (2011), '*African Health Care in India*' in South-South Co-operation: Africa on the Centre Stage, International Political Economy Series, New York: Palgrave Macmillan.

New African Magazine (2012a), '*Pharmaceuticals: India's Generics Flow into Africa*', African Business, 19th January, Available at: <http://africanbusinessmagazine.com/special-reports/other-reports/africa-india-a-partnership-made-in-heaven/pharmaceuticals-indias-generics-flow-into-africa> (Accessed on 07/02/2013).

New African Magazine (2012b), '*Indian Company Take Firm Grip in Africa*', African Business, 19th January, Available at: <http://africanbusinessmagazine.com/special-reports/sector-reports/the-pharmaceutical-industry-in-africa/indian-company-take-firm-grip-in-africa> (Accessed on 07/02/2013).

New African Magazine (2012c), '*African Firms Up For the Fight*', African Business 19th January, Available at: http://africanbusinessmagazine.com/special-reports/sector-reports/the-pharmaceutical-industry-in-africa/african-firms-up-for-the-figh (Accessed on 07/02/2013).

New African Magazine (2012d), '*Fast Growing Belies Small Size*', African Business, 19th January, Available at: http://africanbusinessmagazine.com/special-reports/sector-reports/the-pharmaceutical-industry-in-africa/fast-growing-belies-small-size (Accessed on 07/02/2013).

MEA Factsheet (2013), '*India and Nigeria Bilateral Relations*', Nigeria – Fact Sheet and Bilateral Co-operation, High Commission of India, in Nigeria, Available at:<http://www.indianhcabuja.com/Nigeria-Fact-Sheet.htm> (Accessed on 07/02/2013).

Nigeria Vision 20:2020 (2010) '*The First National Implementation Plans (2010-2013)*', Vol. II: Sectroal Plans and Programmes, Available at: <http://www.npc.gov.ng/vault/files/NV2020-NIP-Volume-II-Originaldocument_ edited__versioin3_10_06_2010.pdf> (Accessed on 07/12/2012).

Nigeria HC. (2013) 'Visiting Nigeria' London, UK, Available at:<http://www.nigeriahc.org.uk/visa-requirements> (Accessed on15/05/2013).

Ojeme, V.V. (2013) 'Primus Hospital Plans Kidney Transplant Centre in Nigeria', Vanguard, 5th March, Available at: <http://www.vanguardngr.com/2013/03/primus-hospital-plans-kidney-transplant-centre-in-nigeria/> (Accessed on 07/02/2013).

PIB (2012), 'India-Africa Science and Technology Ministers Two Day Conference Concludes with a Joint Declaration', Government of India, Available at: <http://pib.nic.in/newsite/erelease.aspx?relid=080683> (Accessed on 07/2/2013).

Placid Way (2012), 'Nigerians Venture to India for Healthcare', Medical Tourism, Available at: <http://www.placidway.com/article/184/Nigerians-Venture-to-India-for-Healthcare> (Accessed on 07/12/2012).

Primus Hospital in Nigeria Profile (2011), 'Overview about Primus', Available at: <http://aboutprimushospital.blogspot.in/> (Accessed on 02/03/2011).

Primus International Super Speciality Hospital (2012), '*Testimonials / Achievements*', Available at: <http://primushospitalnigeria.com/achievements.htm> (Accessed on 27/05/2013).

Prohaska, A. (2012), 'China Poses Major Threat to Indian Pharma Industry Pharmexcil', Austrian Tribune Online Services, 20th December, Available at: <http://austriantribune. com/informationen/121091-china-poses-major-threat-indian-pharma-industry-pharmexcil> (Accessed on 07/02/2013).

Rau, B. S. and Appaji, P.V. (2012), '*Global Pharmaceutical Trade and Contribution of India*', The Pharma Review, 12th January, February, Available at: <http://pharmexcil.org/uploadfile/ufiles/3GlobalPharma TradeContribution India01 jan2012.pdf> (Accessed on 07/2/2012).

SAFPI (2013), '*Nigeria to Host Special African Health Summit in July*', South African Foreign Policy Initiative, Star Africa, Available at: <http://www.safpi.org/news/article/2013/nigeria-host-special-african-health-summit-july> (Accessed on 27/05/2013).

Sen, A. Singh, K. (2012), '*India Eyes $40 billion Global Generic Market; Patents Held by MNCs to expire in over 3 years*',

The Economic Times, 5th October, Available at: <http://articles.economictimes.indiatimes.com/2012-1005/news/34279689_1_indian-generics-japanese-pharma-market-indian-companies> (Accessed on 07/02/2013).

Sonkar, M. (2011), *'Indian Doctors Remove Embedded Bullet from Nigerian Man'*, Medical Times: Aala Times Media Private Limited, 19th July, Available at: http://www.aalatimes.com/2011/07/19/indian-doctors-remove-embedded-bullet-from-nigerian-man/ (Accessed on 19/07/2012).

This Day Live (2010), *'India Condemns Nigerian Bombing'*, Leaders and Company Limited, 4th October, Available at: <http://www.thisdaylive.com/articles/india-condemns-nigerian-bombing/77428/> (Accessed on 07/12/2012).

WHO (2009), 'Nigeria Country Co-operation Strategy: at a Glance', Available at: <http://www.who.int/countryfocus/cooperation_strategy/ccsbrief_nga_en.pdf> (Accessed on 27/05/2013).

WHO (2011), 'The Abuja Declaration: Ten Years on', Available at: http://www.who.int/healthsystems/publications/Abuja10.pdf (Accessed on 27/05/2012).

WHO (2012), *'Cause-specific mortality and morbidity'*, Available at: < http://www.who.int/healthinfo/EN_WHS2012_Part3.pdf > (Accessed on 27/05/2012).

WHO (2013), *'Health Expenditure'*, World Health Statistics, Table -7, Available at:<http://www.who.int/gho/publications/world_health_statistics/EN_WHS2013_Full.pdf> (Accessed on 27/05/2013).

Zee News Limited (2009), *'India`s First Successful Swap Liver Transplant'*, Available at: <http://zeenews.india.com/news/health/health-news/india-s-first-successful-swap-liver-transplant_5093.html> (Accessed on 07/12/2012).

Footnotes

1. The Indigenous Cultural Competency (ICC), Country Coordinating Mechanism (CCM), Health Systems Forum,

Malaria Partnership; Integrated Maternal Newborn and Child Health (IMNCH) partnership are examples. In some states, partners (including Department for International Development (DFID), Canadian International Development Agency (CIDA), the UN System, USAID and the World Bank) are working under the leadership of the State governments towards what might eventually be a Health Sector-Wide Approach (SWAP) (WHO 2009).

2. There is also a plan to set up 500-bed hospitals in Dar es Salaam to serve patients from East and West Africa, which will require an investment of $70m. Apollo Hospitals report that around 35,000 African patients have already travelled to India to get treatment in their hospitals. Indians offers world class medical facilities in world class hospitals and the doctors are comparable with their counterparts in western countries (Akinboade, 2012).

3. The hospital has state of the art departments and eminent surgeons/consultants from across the world. The hospital has started with an aim to deliver the most ethical and compassionate medical care to the nationals of Nigeria (Infinities 2012: pp. 62-63).

4. Primus International Super Specialty Hospital in Nigeria has opened up following departments: Orthopaedics and joint replacement, Spine Surgery, General, Laparoscopic and Bariatric Surgery, Endourology, Reconstructive Urology and Kidney Transplant, Internal Medicine, Paediatrics, Dialysis, Radiology, and Pathology (Infinities 2012: pp. 62-63).

5. Also, with requirement of an investment of $70 m, there is a plan to set up a 500-bed hospital in Dar-es-Salaam to serve patients from East and West Africa. Apollo Hospitals report that around 35,000 African patients have already travelled to India to get treatment in their hospitals. Several Apollo Hospitals in India were the first in the country to receive international healthcare accreditation, being approved by the prestigious US-based JCI (New African Magazine, 2012a).

6. Cipla is the one of the largest exporters of pharmaceutical products from India, exporting Australian Pharmaceutical

Industries (API) and formulation products to over 170 countries (Cipla, 1935). This includes the US, Canada and countries in Europe, Africa, Australasia, Latin America and the Middle East (Cipla, 1935).

7. The company's shares gained 31 per cent. It is considered the fastest growing of South Africa's top 10 pharmaceutical giants and the third biggest pharmaceutical firm in the country. Cipla is currently investing $ 36 m in upgrading its plant in Durban city (New African Magazine, 2012b).

8. In 2001, Cipla, for example, won considerable goodwill when it committed to drastically dropping the price of its ARVs, from over $10,000 a year to less than $400 (New African Magazine, 2012 b).

9. Generic drugs are identical or bio-equivalent to branded drugs in all respect, including safety, strength and quality as it has the same chemical composition (Sen: *The Economic Times*, 2012).

4

Capacity Building in Education: ICT and IT Sectors

India's economic partnership with African countries has been vibrant and extends beyond trade and investment, technology transfers, knowledge sharing, and skills development. This chapter reviews the trends in India–Africa trade and examines Africa's potential for attracting Indian investments in the Information and Communications Technology (ICT) and related sector education sector (The African Development Bank, 2011: p. 8). It also provides an overview of investments and cooperation in developing sectors such as ICT, education, capacity building, and skills transfer in the ICT and Information Technology (IT) sectors.

India is one of the fastest growing IT markets in the world. The rapid emergence of Indian IT sector has played a significant role in transforming India's image from a slow moving bureaucratic economy to a land of innovative entrepreneurs. More recently, online retailing, cloud computing and e-commerce are emerged as the major growth drivers in the sector. The market size of IT in India is expected to touch $ 44.8 billion in

2014 as compared to $ 35.1 billion in 2012, as per International Data Corporation (IDC) (OIFC 2013).

It also assesses India's recent economic and technology boom and the relevant lessons that can be learned by Africa's nascent technological firms and services (The African Development Bank 2011, p. 1). ICT can be broadly viewed under two sectors, IT and ICT. IT is the use of computers and software to manage information. Different companies refer to this corporate function as Management Information Services (MIS) or Information Services (IS). The IT department would be responsible for storing information, protecting information, processing the information, transmitting the information as necessary, and later retrieving information as necessary (Gentile 2012, p. 2).

ICT is electronic technologies used for information storage and retrieval. Their development is partly determined by the ability to establish a synergistic interaction between technological innovation and human values (Adomi and Kpangban, 2010). Capacity building, skills development, transfer of technology and sharing of experiences form an integral part of India's development partnership and co-operation with the developing world. India has been a partner of Nigeria and helped augment its capacity in ICT through the government and private sectors. Government programmes such as the Indian Technical and Economic Co-operation Programme (ITEC) and Special Commonwealth Assistance for Africa Programme (SCAAP) run by the Ministry of External Affairs (MEA), has attracted a steady increase in the number of participants from Africa over the years. The programmes serve as major tools of development partnership assistance by India under the South-South Co-operation (SSC) framework (MEA, 2012b).

The private sector companies such as NIIT, APTECH are contributing to the development of education in the ICT sector in Nigeria. ICT is also accommodating to develop the knowledge economy in Nigeria.

Knowledge Economy in Nigeria

The Nigerian Knowledge Economy (KE) has been always been central to development and can mean the difference between poverty and wealth. The Knowledge Economy was about establishing high tech industries and creating an innovative and entrepreneurial culture. Literature indicates that by adopting existing technologies widely available in developed countries productivity and economic growth can be dramatically boosted (Radwan and Pellegrini: The World Bank, 2010: pp. 1-7).

The Knowledge Economy issues that confront Nigeria and offer policy prescriptions that were allowed the country. And also advantage of the opportunities available in moving towards knowledge-based economy. The Knowledge Assessment Methodology (KAM) developed by the World Bank considers four pillars:

1. Skills and education.
2. Business environment.
3. Information and communications infrastructure.
4. Innovation system.

The ICT backbone was an absolute requisite for a functioning knowledge economy. Nigerians need to be able to communicate with one another and access the internet for business purposes. Currently, the internet provides access to almost the entire spectrum of human knowledge. But it was also a conduit for business services and a channel to market for Nigeria's software developers and other IT-enabled services. Access to landlines has deteriorated and internet access remains costly, with bandwidth severely limited. Only when bandwidth was increased and its cost has been reduced the stage set for all other areas, such as e-government, computer ownership, and internet usage, to flourish. The federal government can promote this evolution by increasing ICT spending, promoting e-government services, subsidising IT training within the government, and promoting ICT literacy in Nigerian schools. Nigeria stands in relation to its competitors in terms of its information infrastructure (*Ibid*, pp. 86-87).

The researcher below discussed the overview of the ICT sector in Nigeria and the cooperative ventures between Nigeria and India to boost IT and ICT.

Overview of the ICT Sector in Nigeria

Nigerian education sector has several shortcomings in the education sector in general and the ICT sector in particular. The prospective that students need computer literacy and knowledge have to be strengthened (Ololube *et.al*. 2009).

The adoption and use of ICT in schools have a positive impact on teaching, learning, and research. Despite the role ICT can play in education, secondary schools in Nigeria have yet to extensively adopt them for teaching and learning at the school level. Efforts geared towards integration of ICT into the secondary school system, have not had much impact. Problems such as poor policy and project implementation strategies and limited information infrastructure militate against these efforts (Adomi and Kpangban, 2010). The main cause for poor ICT penetration and usage among Nigerians is the lack of basic ICT infrastructure as a result of a lack of electricity to power the ICT materials and poor telecommunication facilities. Several cities and rural areas in Nigeria still have fluctuation in their supply of electricity which makes the implementation of ICT in education most difficult. In addition poor economic conditions and their effect on middle level manpower stand as a major barrier to the implementation of ICTs in higher education. Even an average middle income earner cannot afford basic technological communication gadgets (Ololube *et.al*, 2009).

In order to ensure that ICT are widely adopted and used in Nigeria's secondary school system, the following efforts need to be taken:

1. Government should ensure that ICT policy statements are translated into reality. An ICT policy implementation commission should be created. This commission should be funded and given the power to provide ICT facilities in the schools and monitor their use;

2. Computer education should be an elective course in high schools. This means only those who elect to take it will have computer education in high school.

3. Efforts should be made by Ministry of Education (at Federal and State levels) to post teachers skilled in ICT to each secondary school to impart ICT skills to the students (Adomi and Kpangban, 2010); and

4. The bottlenecks that impede the proper implementation of ICT programmes due to lack of funding and trained teachers needs to be addressed.

Thus, for most Nigerian students and faculty members, computers are a luxury in institutions, offices and homes. This has made the integration of necessary online resources (e-mail, world-wide-web, etc.) (Ololube *et al*, 2009).[14] However, the significance of ICT driving the transformation of Africa cannot be understated.

Acknowledging the fact that the government of Nigeria has spelt out its priorities and strategies in its vision document 20:2020.

Nigeria's New Vision: ICT Sector

The government of Nigeria's document "New Vision 20:2020" seeks to attain an information and knowledge-based economy and society that are efficient and technology enabled through a globally competitive ICT industry. The objectives, strategies and targets are as follows:

Objectives

1. Develop sufficient, efficient and affordable ICT infrastructure to accelerate and sustain economic growth and development.

2. Engender rapid ICT penetration and diffusion for efficient and affordable service across the socio-economic sectors of Nigeria.

3. Develop globally competitive indigenous human capital and knowledge-based products and services in targeted areas of ICT (software, hardware, networks, card technologies, security or biometrics, web and digital content development, etc).

4. Deploy ICT in government for transparency and accountability as well as to enhance efficiency, effectiveness and increase government capacity to deliver citizen centred services to attain national competitiveness.

5. Promote Research and Development (R and D) activities to stimulate and sustain innovation in ICT solutions; and

6. Develop the ICT industry for the production of software and hardware to global standards.

Strategies

7. Facilitate increased awareness of potential of ICT by literate people in rural and urban-areas of the country.

8. Promote the personal acquisition and ownership of computers by pupils, students, employees and households, local adaptations of foreign ICT systems and solutions that do not infringe patent rights through support and incentives, development of local software that interface with Nigerian languages in either voice-text or text-voice modes.

9. Put in place a functional educational curricula for Early Childhood Care and Development (ECCDE) primary, secondary and tertiary levels with appropriate ICT skills content and is ICT driven content philosophy by 2010.

10. Provide recognition for non-formal and distance e-learning modes of education and enact enabling legislation for e-Government, e.g., Digital Signature Act, provide policies and fiscal incentives to encourage ICT hardware manufacturers to invest towards improving the amount of local content in their products and services.

11. Make the use of basic and specialised work-related ICT skills a requirement for employment and advancement in Media Development Authority (MDAs) by 2010.

12. Strengthen the competencies and capabilities of researchers and research institutes and tertiary institutions to be globally competitive in targeted ICT areas and provide high tech equipment and internet connectivity for all institutions; and

13. Facilitate linkage between national research institutes and tertiary institutions with internationally recognised ICT-based research institutes abroad.

Targets

14. Attain tele density of 65 per cent from the present 47 per cent by 2013 and achieve 60 per cent ICT literacy among the literate population by 2013.

15. Achieve a ratio of computer scientists, engineers and technologists to population of 1:10,000 by 2013 and achieve 30 per cent of Nigerian content in ICT hardware, software and services by 2013.

16. Build capacity of 40 per cent of the workforce to acquire basic and work-relevant ICT skills 2013; and achieve 1:5 ratio of personnel to computer for 40 per cent of the workforce by 2013.

17. Achieve computerisation of 30 per cent of the business processes of MDAs by 2013 and achieve a ratio of computer scientists, engineers and technologists to population of 1:10,000 by 2013.

18. Achieve 30 per cent of Nigerian content in ICT hardware, software and services by 2013 and achieve three per cent contribution by the ICT sector to GDP by 2013; and

19. Achieve at least 0.1 per cent of GDP investment in ICT R and D annually to improve local software and hardware capacity (Nigeria Vision, 20:2020 2010).

Africa is one of the fastest growing markets worldwide in ICT adoption and communication technology. It has the potential of becoming one of the most important markets for the Indian IT industry. Governments and businesses that were apprehensive till some time back have realised the potential of ICT and are therefore willing to invest in this sector (Infinities, 2013, p. 53). Indian companies have made a significant contribution to Nigeria's endeavour to build a knowledge economy by capacity building through ICT and IT sector in Africa.

Capacity Building by India in Africa: ICT and IT

India's booming economy, its public and private sector's investment overseas and leadership in science and technology has shaped its policy towards Africa. As such, India is focused on intensifying economic and commercial ties whilst contributing to development of African countries through cooperation and technical assistance, including in the IT and ICT sectors (The African Development Bank, 2011, p. 1).

Africa's IT market was headed for growth in 2011-12, and market levels are expected to reach $ 26.53 billion by 2014. It is setting in motion a number of key trends that have reshaped the IT landscape in Africa (Infinities, 2013: p. 53). IT-based economic growth in India could help African countries. The people in sub-Saharan Africa could be the major beneficiaries as ICT can help bridge the digital divide and improve their competitiveness in the global marketplace. India and sub-Saharan Africa come together with the inflows of private sector investments in this area. The Indian experience in information technology, tele-communications sector, and research-based development could be transferred to African countries through the ITEC programme and Indian private and public sectors investments in Africa (The African Development Bank, 2011: p. 8).

Other development co-operation instruments are the specialised capacity building programmes mainly the ITEC and SCAAP. These tools were established to promote cooperation and partnership for mutual benefit, and include training activities such as feasibility studies and consultancy services, deputations of Indian experts abroad, study tours and aid for disaster relief (Hoogcarspel, 2011: p. 59). In 2009-10, India provided assistance worth $ 16.8 million under ITEC, $ 1.8 million under SCAAP, and $ 24.6 million as direct aid to African countries (The African Development Bank, 2011: p. 1).

Thrust in Nigeria: ICT and IT Sectors

The growth of Information Technology and Business Process Outsourcing sector (IT-BPO) are transforming a country's economy and improve the lives of its citizens. For example, India, has achieved a phenomenal growth in IT-BPO sector. During 2010, India could boast of a 64 per cent share of globally off-shored IT services and also 37 per cent share in IT-Enabled Services (ITES). Several African countries want to invest in IT and ITES to boost employment and economic growth (World Bank, 2013a).

The major thrust of the IT policy in Nigeria, the vision of the policy is to make Nigeria IT-capable country in Africa and a key player in the information society by the year 2015, using IT as the engine for sustainable development and global competitiveness are;

1. Education
2. Creation of wealth
3. Poverty alleviation
4. Job creation, and
5. Global competitiveness (Nwabueze and Ozioko, 2011).

African leaders recognise that India has a great deal of knowledge to share to help guide policies, investment in skills development. Complementing the World Bank's New Economy Skills for Africa Programme: Information and Communication Technologies (NESAP-ICT), the South-South facility funded a knowledge exchange for 54 policymakers and stakeholders from Ghana, Kenya, Madagascar, Mozambique, Nigeria, Rwanda, Senegal and Tanzania, to visit India (World Bank, 2013a).

This exchange raised awareness of IT/ITES approaches and policies leading to implementation of specific strategies for strengthening the IT/ITES sector and each participating country developed an Action Plan, which has led to concrete steps to support ongoing skills development initiatives and ICT institutions in nearly all countries (*Ibid*).

Each of the eight countries identified representatives from government, learning institutions. And also the private sector to travel to Mumbai, Hyderabad, and Bangalore. The delegates visited IT companies, industry associations, and BPO entrepreneurs, ICT skills development and educational institutions, and the Indian Ministry of Education. These organisations and individuals shared insights regarding the future of ITES. It's potential to create employment and specific strategies to support ICT sector growth and enter global value chains (*Ibid*).[15]

The participating countries expanded on country Action Plans, articulating a vision and strategy for developing IT/ITES markets in each country. These plans have led to a number of concrete ICT sector skills development initiatives in Nigeria was the World Bank supported pilot in Nigeria to assess and certify skills for the BPO industry. The next section is divided into two sections namely:

1. The role of the Indian government in Nigeria's ICT and IT sector.

2. The role of the Indian private sector in Nigeria's ICT and IT sector.

The Role of the Indian Government in Nigeria's ICT and IT Sectors

The Indian information and communication technology industry has witnessed excellent growth in the past two decades. Capitalising on its advantages of talent pool, lower cost of operation and the innovative remote delivery model, India has established itself as a global leader in the ICT sector (OIFC, 2013).

India's Capabilities in the IT Sector

The increase in IT investments by Indian Small and Medium Enterprises (SME) indicates constant progress in business maturity levels. India was home to about 200 wholly owned IT and ITES centres of multinational companies and the most preferred offshore destination as compared to 120 other offshoring locations across the globe. The cabinet has recently approved the National Policy on Information Technology (NPIT) 2012, which aims to leverage ICT to address the country's economic and developmental challenges (*Ibid*). Some of the thrust areas of the policy include:

1. To increase revenues of IT and ITES (Information Technology Enabled Services) Industry from $ 100 billion currently to $ 300 billion by 2020 and expand exports from $ 69 billion currently to $ 200 billion by 2020.

2. To encourage adoption of ICTs in key economic and strategic sectors to improve their competitiveness and productivity.

3. To gain significant global market-share in emerging technologies and services.

4. To provide fiscal benefits to– SME and startups for adoption of IT in value creation.

5. To create a pool of 10 million additional skilled manpower in ICT.

6. To make at least one individual in every household e-literate.

7. To promote innovation and (R and D) in cutting edge technologies and development of applications and solutions in areas like localisation, location-based services, mobile value added services, cloud computing, social media and utility models; and

8. To make India the global hub for development of language technologies, to encourage and facilitate development of content accessible in all Indian languages and thereby help bridge the digital divide (*Ibid*).

According to India's National Knowledge Commission, India would experience a knowledge revolution which can be seen by the dramatic revolution in the field of Information and Technology. IT comprises of wide range of activities like Office Automation, Telecommunication and Computing (ATC), therefore provides job avenues for those who have acquired the right qualifications for it. In the beginning of this millennium, National Association of Software and Services Companies (NASSC) made estimation that India would require 10,00,000 trained software professionals. The present availability of such skilled people is only five per cent of the required amount. And this sector is going to provide employment to a large number of such professionals. Specialised field of IT requires academic and technical skills accordingly (*Ibid*). Many diploma and degrees courses are there for those who have an aptitude and flair for the subject. These are:

1. Bachelor in Computer Applications (BCA);
2. Bachelor in Science with Computers (B.Sc.);
3. Masters in Computer Applications (MCA);
4. M.Sc. in computers.

5. Masters in System Management;

6. B. Tech. and B.E.;

7. M. Tech.;

8. Diploma in Computer Applications;

9. Post Graduate Diploma in Computer Applications (*Ibid*).

Financial Assistance

In financial assistance whiles the underlying topic of 2010 was recovery in emerging markets. Worldwide spending in IT products and services increased significantly in 2011 and the same year India's growth has reflected new demand for IT goods and services and a major surge in the use of private and public cloud, mobile computing on a variety of devices and through a range of new software applications. The high inflow of Foreign Direct Investment (FDI) in the IT sector, and huge volumes of FDI in the IT industry of India has not only boosted the industry but the entire Indian economy. In May 2011, FDI inflow rose by more than 100 per cent to $ 4.66 billion, up from $ 2.21 billion. This is the highest monthly inflow in 39 months. Foreign technology induction is also encouraged both through FDI and through foreign technology collaboration agreements. Greater transparency in policies and procedures has made India an investor. A foreign company can hold equity in Indian company upto 100 per cent (FICCI website).

Nigeria has benefited from India's private and public sector companies that offer IT and ICT solutions.

Nigeria Benefit from India's Private and Public Sectors

The annual Information Technology Association of Nigeria (ITAN) and National Association of Computer and Software Companies of India, (NASSCOM) Business Summit tagged 'ITAN CEO-NASSCOM 2012'. More than 20 leading ICT companies from India have attending the event representing a significant identification with Nigeria's government transformational agenda for the ICT sector and ITAN's new stance to build international partnership to grow the local industry. ITAN and NASSCOM benefit from international business and professional membership of Nigeria and India. NASSCOM was the premier trade body and the "Chamber of Commerce" for the IT-BPO industry in India and ITAN was the premier trade industry group for ICT companies in Nigeria (Tooki: Business World, 2012).

The local ICT organisations to synergise and collaborate among key international ICT players and creating education opportunities, influencing policy formulations in information communication technologies development, promotion and enhancement of the Nigerian ICT industry with other relevant stakeholders. The local ICT companies currently deserve a lot of private and public sector support in terms of increasing their demand for goods and services supplied, and engendering adequate partnership to promoting local content. Indian software and several ICT companies have very strong presence in Nigeria. Investment from India into Africa was in excess of several billion dollars and the Indian government further pledged to invest hundreds of millions of dollars into African initiatives and training focusing on ICT; the government total pledge for all economic and trade activities for the entire continent was in excess of $ five billion line of credit. The ITAN, NASCOM CEOs forum offers a strong plank for industry leaders of the two countries to explore ways of mutually growing businesses particularly as it concerns the ICT sector (*Ibid*).

In IAFS, the given a boost to ICT and IT with countries in Africa. Given its proven expertise in the ICT and IT sectors, India can replicate its successful experience and capabilities in the ICT sector in Nigeria.

India-Africa Forum Summits

Recognising that IT is emerging as one of the major vehicles of economic growth and has become fundamental part of infrastructure and improvement of myriad sectors of socio-economic activities, Africa and India agreed to take following steps:

1. Co-operation and information sharing among ICT regulatory bodies;

2. Development of ICT tools and applications aimed at improving public administration at different levels of government, taxation management, public financing and delivery of public services;

3. Promotion of co-operation in the range of non-material knowledge-based human resources such as technology, organiszation, information, education and skills development; and

4. Co-operation in setting up community information centers using IT to accelerate socio-economic development, with a view to providing rural connectivity and bridging the digital divides (IAFS, 2008);

5. In 2011 ICT, recognising the contribution made by IT to the economic development of Africa and India;

6. India will established an India-Africa Institute of Information Technology (IIT) which would bridge the gap between academia and industry, and serve as a think-tank for the professional development of IT and provide capacity building and education for the growth of IT in Africa; and

7. *India will support the African Union's initiative in this sector and support capacity building to this end through the ITEC (programme* (IAFS, 2011).

In C.V. Raman Fellowship, the process aims to provide an opportunity for enhanced capacity building of African researchers and creating avenues for partnerships and future collaboration among research and academic institutions of both India and Africa regions. (Department of Science and Technology, G.O.I 2011)

C.V. Raman Fellowship

The programme intended to strengthen scientific co-operation between India and Africa by providing fellowships to African researchers for undertaking advanced scientific work in leading science and technology institutions, across India. African researchers have praised the fellowship as being mutually beneficial to both India and Africa (*Ibid*).

Under the ITEC/SCAAP programme, civilians from all over Africa including Nigeria can apply for scholarships in Indian educational institutions. In 2009-10, Nigeria was able to utilise 85 out of 100 allotted fellowships. The 130 seat ITEC quota for Nigeria for the year 2010-11 were fully utilised. Following the second Africa-India Forum Summit of 2011, Nigeria's ITEC quota for 2011-12 has been further increased by 190 to 177 and full utilisation was anticipated. The 130 seat Indian Technical and Economic Co-operation (ITEC) quota for Nigeria for the year 2010-11 was fully utilised. Following the second Africa-India Forum Summit, Nigeria's ITEC quota for 2011-12 was increased to 190 and an overwhelming 177 slots were utilised. During 2012-13, all 210 slots were utilised (MEA, 2014: p. 3).

The Commissioner of Human Resources, Science and Technology of African Union Commission, Prof. Jean-Pierre

Ezin said that "delighted and deeply honoured to have this opportunity to welcome this distinguished gathering of Ministers and delegates for the India-Africa Science and Technology Ministerial Conference and Tech Expo. India has offered more than 700 C.V. Raman Scientific Fellowships till 2014. So far more than 150 post-doctorates from Africa have availed the fellowships. This would help in building capacity for scientific research in Africa. As per India's commitment to assist African countries in the field of Science and Technology, proposals for institutional strengthening of identified institutions in Africa and transfer of need-based technologies have also been initiated" (MEA, 2012b).

The C.V. Raman International Research Fellowship for African Researchers has completed two years of its implementation and is turning out to be a big hit, with 134 candidates from 30 African nations availing it against last two calls (2010 and 2011). African researchers have praised the fellowship as being mutually beneficial to both India and Africa, according to the observations received from them. The fellowship covers travel expenses to India apart from providing monthly allowance up to Rs 50,000. For applications under C.V. Raman Fellowship programme was advertised in March 2012. In total 403 applications from various African countries were received against the call for which last date was September 30, 2012. Based on scientific merit, number of slots for the country, compatibility of the proposed research work with the host Indian Institute, Department of Science and Technology has awarded this prestigious 'C.V. Raman International Fellowship for African Researchers' to the following candidates. In addition four applications are under processing (Department of Science and Technology, G.O.I., 2012).

The selected candidates are being informed separately to complete administrative formalities to avail this award in Nigeria country is as follows:

Nigeria 4.1: CV Raman International Fellowship for Nigerian Researchers (2010)

S.No.	*Name of Candidates Parent*	*Institute*	*Host Institute*
1.	Bukola Olanike Oyebanji	Obafemi Awolowo University	Jaypee University of Information Technology, Waknaghat, Distt. Solan Himachal Pradesh (HP)
2.	Johnson Ozoemenam Urama	University of Nigeria	Tata Institute of Fundamental Research, Pune
3.	Fabian I. Ezema	University of Nigeria	Shivaji University, Kolhapur

Source: Department of Science and Technology, GoI 2010.

Africa recognised the important contribution made by the Pan-African E-Network Project to the continent's efforts to improve the sector and that this was necessary in order to bridge the digital divide. The Pan-African-e-Network, develop Tele-Education learning centres in India, Nigeria and other African country.

Pan-African e-Network: India Africa Tele-Education

The Pan-African e-Network project was to assist Africa in capacity building by way of imparting quality education to 10,000 students in Africa over a five year period in various disciplines from some of the best Indian Universities/Educational Institution (Pan-African-e-Network Project Phase 2). The project aims to create significant linkages for tele-education making available the facilities and expertise of some of the best universities in India to the people of Africa. Regarding Tele-Education services from India, more than 2000 students from Africa have been enrolled in five different top ranking universities in India in various disciplines like Master of Business Administration (MBA), Master in Finance Control, and Post Graduate (PG) Diploma in IT, Master of Science (M.Sc.) in IT and Bachelor in Finance and Investment Analysis and many others. Regular Tele-education live sessions are being conducted from India and students have shown great interest in the courses. Tele-communications Consultants India Ltd. (TCIL) has established the network with a Data Centre in TCIL Bhawan, New Delhi that acts as a gateway to the Hub Station in Dakar for connectivity of Indian institutions on the African side (Pan-African E-Network Project Phase 2).

Under the Tele-education part, 9960 students from African countries have already registered with Indian universities and are being imparted Tele-education by Indian universities. 3577 tele-education sessions and 465 Tele-Medicine consultations had also taken place till October 2012 (MEA Annual Report, 2012-13, p. 62).

Tele-education teaching centres have already been set-up in the five Indian Universities, namely; Amity University, (NOIDA); New Delhi (IGNOU); Pilani (BITS); University of Delhi; University of Madras. Forty-seven Learning Centres (LCs) have already been set up in African countries (MEA, 2013).

Tele-education learning centres have been set-up in the five Regional University Centres in Africa, namely, Kwame Nkrumah (University of Science and Technology), Ghana; (Makerere University), Uganda; (Yaoundé University), Cameroon; (Alexandria Faculty of Commerce), Egypt; (Chancellor College), Zambia, Malawi. 9916 students from African countries have already registered with Indian universities for a variety of PG, Under-Graduate (UG) and certificate courses. 3503 tele-education sessions have been held till end September 2012 (*Ibid*).

On February 26, 2009, at the inauguration of Pan-African e-Network Project at TCIL, New Delhi by then Enterprise Asset Management (EAM), Pranab Mukherjee, was attended by Prof Dora Akunyili, Nigerian Minister of Information and Communication at the Learning Centre, University of Lagos (*Ibid*).

From the Indian private sector there are the several technology institutes set up in Nigeria to offer education in the ICT and IT sector. These are the NIIT and APTECH centre. The researcher tried to explain the role of ICT and IT sector along with private sector in Nigeria.

The Role of the Indian Private Sector in Nigeria's: ICT and IT Sector

The NASSCOM of India was in Nigeria to seek collaboration with the ITAN on local content development in ICT. Those who attended the business summit between both associations discussed various areas of partnership relating to technology transfers, domestication, deployment of local talent by Indian firms and the need to support growth of local IT entrepreneurs (Okwuke: Daily Independent, 2012).

Indian ICT was investing $ 2 million in Nigeria, part of which was for setting up a training centre. The training centre in New Delhi has over 150 certified trainers in different fields from different vendors as their trainers, while Microsoft, Oracle and Cisco are some of the world's leading vendors who partner with Koenig Solutions Limited, an IT company. The company decided to invest in Nigeria because of the huge market and opportunities in the country and assured that with the establishment of a qualitative training centre in Nigeria to enable more Nigerians would be certified in ICT training. The company Koenig Solutions Limited was rated one of the top 100 companies in India. It assured that the trainees would benefit immensely from the knowledge of different professionals in the ICT Company. Indian ICT firms seek new opportunities in Nigeria. Their investments in ICT in excess of N3 trillion within the last eight years (2005-2012) Nigeria was clearly investors' preferred destination. In line with this, about 20 leading Indian ICT firms came into the country. Indians were seeking new business opportunities in Nigeria's burgeoning ICT industry (Williams: Business Day, 2012).

For Indian IT companies to operate in Nigeria, they also need to have a local partner in Nigeria to front end their business (Infinities, 2013: p. 54). Indian IT companies are playing a major role in the development of this sector in Nigeria. There are two major Indian institutes that offer IT training in Nigeria. They are as follows:

1. NIIT
2. APTECH

1. National Institute of Information Technology (NIIT)

NIIT, is the leading Global Talent Development Corporation and Asia's largest IT trainer, to enable meritorious students seek a career in the fast growing IT sector in the country.[16] It aims to create a skilled workforce for the Nigerian IT industry. It also offers the NIIT Nigeria Scholarship which will help students to get skilled for a Global career in IT through training in

Map showing the location of NIIT and APTECH centres in Nigeria

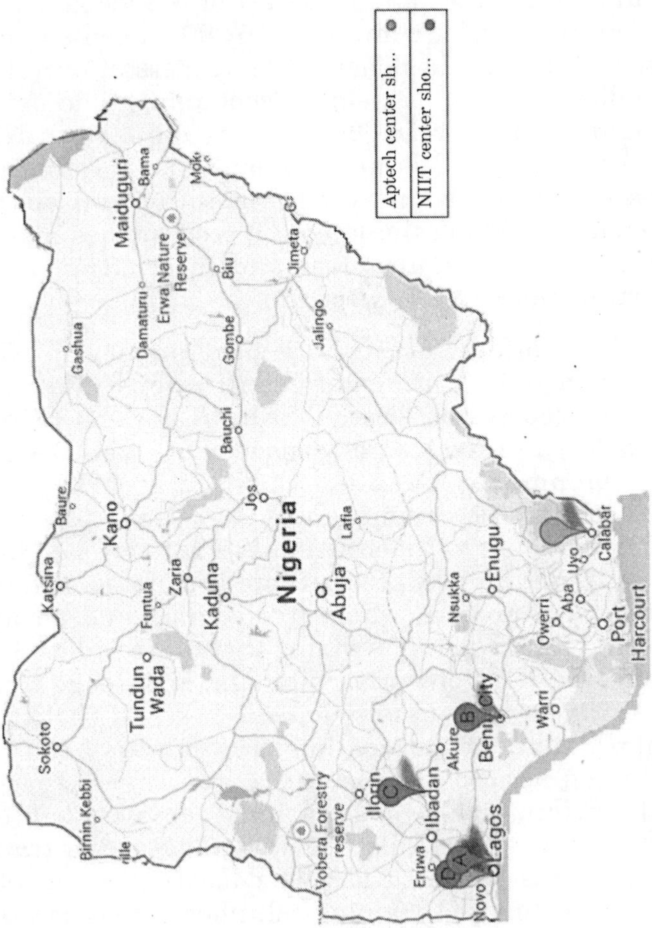

Source: Google Map.

technology. According to industry sources, "IT industry in Nigeria was estimated to be among the fastest growing IT industries in the world. NIIT conducts the IT Scholarship yearly to help find meritorious students to join this industry and be a part of the global skilled IT talent pool". NIIT trains over 16,000 students in Nigeria every year and has shaped the careers of over 120,000 students in past 13 years (Scholarships and Jobs.com, 2013). With over 16,000 students enrolled in Nigeria, every year NIIT is acknowledged as the undisputed leader in the country's IT training and education segment, offering the latest IT programmes mapped to the industry requirement and international vendor certifications (NIIT, website).

NIIT offers cutting-edge programmes in Nigeria, mapped to international certifications- Mastermind Series, courses on Oracle, Java, CCNA and CCNP, A+ and N+, Infrastructure Management, Web Design and Development, Graphic Designing, MIS, Project Management, among others. The Indian High Commissioner to Nigeria, Mahesh Sachdev said his visit was to inform AkwaIbom State graduates of the NIIT admission process, where free courses and airfare are available for Nigerians willing to study in India. Sachdev said "the NIIT offers learning and knowledge solutions globally to individuals, enterprises and institutes in informative technology, business process outsourcing, banking finance and insurance, executive management education, school education, communicable and professional life skills and vocational skills training". In Nigeria, NIIT provides IT education to individuals; offers customised training solutions for corporate; and cater to the IT learning needs of university and school students (Voice of Nigeria, 2013).

2. *APTECH Centers*

APTECH Nigeria training processes focus on continuous value addition to its intellectual and knowledge resources. By giving unlimited access to the latest in technology, APTECH Nigeria helps its people stay at the leading edge of technical and soft skills (Aptech, 2011).

Currently, Aptech centres have over 400 computers deployed within the country for training and are in the process of adding additional capacity. In addition to the traditional Instructor-led Training, all centres are configured to provide online training and online examinations (Aptech, 2011). APTECH has delivered training to over 20,000 individuals in Nigeria in a wide range of courses from basic appreciation courses to high-end Software Engineering and Networking programmes (*Ibid*).

Critical Assessment

The ICT revolution in Nigeria as stated in the ICT Policy was yet to attain the critical mass required to make the necessary impact on teaching, learning, and student/teacher populations all over Nigeria. The impact or activities of the National Information Technology Development Agency (NITDA), Exchange-Traded Fund (ETF), net, banking institutions and providers have been recognised in moving the country toward the realisation of its ICT vision. ICT facilities and infrastructures are yet to be widely provided; neither are there full Internet services in all the government parastatals as stipulated in the strategic plan for achieving the ICT vision. As of 2011, the secondary and primary schools are yet to attain the 500,000 skilled personnel in ICT (Sofowora, 2012).

The challenges facing the utilisation and diffusion of ICT in education in Nigeria are:

1. Techno-phobia resulting in poor utilisation, general misunderstanding of ICT as part of administration.

2. Lack of commitment on the part of the government.

3. Epileptic power supply.

The following recommendations are made to ensure effective implementation of ICT policy.

1. There should be a policy at the ministerial level to help coordinate all the ICT programmes and projects being implemented separately in the education sector so as to reduce wastage and duplication.

2. The low percentage of teachers with ICT skills and the challenges of the ICT education drive needed must be given high priority.

3. Government must provide enough budget and special ICT fund as stipulated in the policy to ensure meaningful provision of these facilities (*Ibid*).

India has played a significant and beneficial role in Nigeria ICT sector. Indian IT professionals are training Nigerians in accountancy, the education sector (Vasudevan, 2012: p. 05). A delegation of the Educational Service Center (ESC) of India was here to explore business tie-ups between Nigerian and Indian entrepreneurs in the electronics and ICT sectors (Kokutse, 2013).

Conclusion

In this chapter India and Nigeria's capacity building in education: ICT and IT Sectors have been analysed. The focus of this chapter was on the capacity building in education sectors between the two countries. India has being engaged in Nigerian education and capacity building sectors mainly through private partnerships. Several Indian ICT and IT firms are active in Nigeria.

Indian Firms also offers and conducting courses to provide business focus knowledge to the Nigerian students as well as professionals. A delegation of the ESC of India was here to explore business tie-ups between Nigerian and Indian entrepreneurs in the electronics and ICT sectors (Kokutse, 2013).

Indo-Africa ICT Partnership, "the Indian government and the council were interested in harnessing the huge Nigeria market" for their made in India ICT products and services. The world today looks forward to India's ICT products and Nigeria as a strategic partner, cannot afford to be left out. There Council was in Nigeria to interact with Nigerian buyers of ICT products and services, as well as explore the possibilities of business cooperation and strategic alliances with them" (Leadership Newspapers Group, 2012).

The delegation leader said they would enter into partnership with Nigerian dealers in providing electronics hardware, information technology services and IT enabled services to Nigerians. As a catalyst for the India's ICT industry, there council was here to develop a new mechanism of making India's ICT products accessible and affordable to Nigerians. With the huge market in Nigeria, more and more Indian ICT companies are willing to extend their high technology solutions to Nigeria. The delegation was in Nigeria to promote trade and investment opportunities between India and Nigeria. ICT development was one new area where India's government and its electronics and computer software export promotion council are seriously looking at promoting trade relations with Nigeria (*Ibid*).

References

Adomi, E. E. and Kpangban, E. (2010), '*Application of ICTs in Nigerian Secondary Schools*', Library Philosophy and Practice, ISSN 1522-0222, Available at: <http://www.webpages.uidaho.edu/~mbolin/adomi-kpangban.htm>(Accessed on 23/05/2013).

Aptech Ltd. (2011), '*Aptech Nigeria*', Available at: <http://www.aptech-ng.com/aptech-nigeria.html> (Accessed on 09/06/2013).

Business Line (2013), '*More Nigerians to Benefit from Indian Fellowship*', The Hindu Business Line 19th December, Available at: http://www.thehindubusinessline.com/news/international/more-nigerians-to-benefit-from-indian-fellowship/article4216322.ece (Accessed on 23/05/2013).

Department of Science and Technology (2011), '*CV Raman International Fellowship for African Researchers*', Government of India, New Delhi, Available at: <http://www.dst.gov.in/whats_new/whats_new12/C_V_Raman_Fellowship_AF_R-2011-2012.pdf> (Accessed on 16/02/2013).

Department of Science and Technology (2012), '*C. V. Raman International Fellowship for African Researchers*', Government of India, New Delhi, Available at: http://www.dst.gov.in/whats_new/whats_new13/Result%20CVRF_2012.pdf (Accessed on 16/02/2013).

FICCI.Com, Available at: http://www.ficci.com/sector/21/Project_docs/FICCI_website_content_-IT.pdf (Accessed on 10/03/2013).

Gentile, S. (2012), '*Project Management in the Information Technology Industry*', Master of Science in Management of Projects and Programs, Rabb School of Continuing Studies Division of Graduate Professional Studies Brandeis University, Available at : <http://projectmgmt.brandeis.edu/downloads/BRU_MSMPP_WP_May2012_Project_Management_Information_Technology_Industry.pdf >(Accessed on 10/07/2013).

Goodie, K. (2013), '*Lack of Educational ICT Behind Nigeria's Stunted S&T Growth*', Biz Tech Africa, 10th May, Available at: http://www.biztechafrica.com/article/lack-educational-ict-behind-nigerias-stunted-st-gr/5993/ (Accessed on 23/05/2013).

GoogleMap, Available at <https://maps.google.co.in/maps?client=firefoxa&q=NIIT+center+sh own+in+nigeria+map&ie=UTF8&ei=_CAF UsmIO8PnrAfp 7IDICA&ved=0CAgQ_AUoAg> (Accessed on 10/07/2013).

Hoogcarspel, J. A. (2011), Securing Natural Resources in a Changing Global Order: The Case of Indo-Nigerian Relations. MSC, Thesis Political Science, International Relations, Universities Van Amsterdam, Available at: <http://epa.iias.asia/files/Jan%20Arne%20Hoogcarspel%20%20Securing %20natural %20resources%20in%20a%20changing% 20global%20order %20the%20case%20of%20Indo-Nigerian%20relations.pdf> (Accessed on 26/02/2013).

IAFS (2008), '*Plan of Action of the Framework for Co-operation on the India Africa Forum Summit*', Addis Ababa, Embassy of India: First IAFS, April 8-9, New Delhi, Available at: <http://www.indianembassy.gov.et/?q=node/21> (Accessed on 26/02/2013).

IAFS (2011) '*Plan of Action of the Framework for Co-operation on the India Africa Forum Summit*', Addis Ababa, Embassy of India: Second IAFS, 25th May, New Delhi, Available at: <http://www.indianembassy.gov.et/?q=node/21> (Accessed on 26/02/2013).

Infinities (2012), '*Focus on India's Ties with Nigeria Benin, Cameroon' and Chad*', Edition, 5th Siddis: the African of India, High Commission of India, Abuja, Available at: http://indianhcabuja.com/docs/InfiniTies_2012_Magazine.pdf(Accessed on 27/05/2013).

Infinities (2013), '*Infinities Focus on India's Ties with Nigeria, Benin, and Cameroon and* Chad', 6th Edition 2013, Available at: <http://www.indianhcabuja.com/docs/InfiniTies2013.pdf> (Accessed on 07/02/2013).

Kokutse, F. (2013), '*Indian Team in Nigeria for Tie-Ups in Electronics, IT Sectors*', Indo Asian News Service, Available at:<http://www.indiaafricaconnect.in/index.php?param=news/5290/india-in-africa/117>(Accessed on 23/05/2013).

Leadership (2012), '*Indian IT Companies to Take Advantage of Nigeria's Market*', Leadership Newspapers Group, 26th November, Available at <http://leadership.ng/nga/articles/41057/2012/11/26/indian_it_ companies_ take_advantage_ nigerias_ market. html> (Accessed on 26/01/2013).

MEA (2012-13), '*Annual Report 2012-2013*', Policy Planning and Research Division, Government of India, New Delhi, Available at: <http://www.mea.gov.in/Uploads/PublicationDocs/21385_Annual_Report_20122013_English.pdf>(Accessed on 10/07/2013).

MEA (2012a), '*Response to a Report in the Guardian Newspaper on Counterfeit Medicines in Africa*', Government of India, New Delhi, Available at: http://www.mea.gov.in/mediabriefings. htm?dtl/21019/Response+to+a+report+in+The+Guardian+newspaper+on+counterfeit+medicines+in+ Africa (Accessed on 30/02/2013).

MEA (2012b), '*India and Nigeria Relations*', Government of India, New Delhi, Available at: <http://www.mea.gov.in/Images/pdf/Nigeria-January-2012.pdf> (Accessed on 26/02/2013).

MEA (2013), '*Pan-African e-Network Project*', Government of India, New Delhi, Available at:<http://mea.gov.in/portal/Fore\ignRelation/Pan_African_e_docx_for_xp.pdf>(Accessed on 07/02/2013).

Nigeria Vision 20:2020 (2010), '*The First National Implementation Plans (2010-2013)*', Vol.II: Sectoral Plans and Programmes, Available at: <http://www.npc.gov.ng/vault/files/NV2020-NIP-Volume-II-Original document_edited__ versioin3_10_06_2010.pdf> (Accessed on 07/12/2012).

NIIT (2013), '*NIIT Announces the 14th I.T.*', Scholarship in Nigeria to Reward Meritorious Students Seeking Global Career in IT, [Online] Available at: <http://www.niit.com/newsandevents/Lists/NIIT%20News/disformCustomv3.aspx?List=a325a1cf-a064-4573-b17a-3ce893a0d178&ID=364#sthash.ZhCemyLv.dpbs> (Accessed on 04/07/2013).

NIIT Website, Available at: <http://www.niitnigeria.com/about.php > (Accessed on 23/05/2013).

Nwabueze, A. U. and Ozioko R. E. (2011), '*Information and Communication Technology for Sustainable Development in Nigeria*', Library Philosophy and Practice, ISSN 15220222, Available at: http://www.webpages.uidaho.edu/~mbolin/nwabueze-ozioko.htm (Accessed on 23/05/2013).

OIFC (2013), '*Information and Communication Technology (ICT) in India*,' Overseas Indian Facilitation Center, 28th June, Available at: <http://www.oifc.in/Sectors/Information-and-Communication-Technology-ICT-in-India> (Accessed on 23/05/2013).

Okwuke, E. (2012), '*ITAN Drives Foreign Direct Investment*', Daily Independent, 25th September, Available at: <http://www.dailyindependentnig.com/2012/09/itan-drives-foreign-direct-investment/> (Accessed on 09/02/2013).

Ololube and *et.al.* (2009), '*Instructional Technology in Higher Education: A Case of Selected Universities in the Niger Delta Previous*', Asia-Pacific Forum on Science Learning and Teaching, Vol. 10, Issue 2, Article 7 Dec. 2009, Available at: <http://www.ied.edu.hk/apfslt/v10_issue2/ololube/ololube3.htm> (Accessedon23/03/201).

PAENP (2012), '*Inauguration of Pan-African e-Network Project (Phase 2)*', Available at :<http://www.panafricanenetwork.com/> (Accessed on 12/12/2013).

Radwan, I, and Pellegrini, G. (2010), '*Knowledge, Productivity, and Innovation in Nigeria Creating a New Economy*', The International Bank for Reconstruction and Development/The World Bank Washington DC, Available at: http://siteresources.worldbank.org/EDUCATION/Resources/278200109907987269/Knowledge_ productivity_ innovation_ Nigeria.pdf (Accessed on 23/05/2013).

Sofowora, O.A. (2012), '*The Diffusion of Information and Communication Technology in Primary Schools in Nigeria: Utilisation and Challenges*', International Journal of Cyber Society and Education, Vol. 5, No. 1, June 2012, Available at: http://academicjournals.org/ojs2/index.php/IJCSE/article/viewFile/940/97 (Accessed on– 23/05/2013).

The African Development Bank (2011), '*India's Economic Engagement with Africa*', Africa Economic Brief, Vol. 2, Issue 6, May 11, pp. 1-8, Available at: http://www.afdb.org/fileadmin/uploads/afdb/Documents/Publications/India%27s% 20Economic %20 Engagement%20with%20Africa.pdf (Accessed on 11/05/2012).

The World Bank (2013a), '*Enhancing Capacity to Build ICT-Sector Skills in Africa*', South-South Knowledge Exchange Hub, Available at: http://wbi.worldbank.org/sske/sske/cases/enhancing-ict-skills-africa (Accessed on 10/07/2013).

Tooki, A. (2012), '*20 Indian IT Companies to Hit Nigeria for Itan / Nascom Summit*', Business World Intelligence, IT World, 17th, Monday, Available at: <http://businessworldng.com/web/articles/2439/1/20-Indian-IT-Companies-to-Hit-Nigeria-for—ItanNascom-Summit/Page1.html> (Accessed on 23/05/2013).

Voice of Nigeria Website (2013), '*AkwaIbom to Partner with India on ICT*', June 29, Available at: http://www.voiceofnigeria.org/Nigeria/Akwa-Ibom-to-partner-with-India-on-ICT.html (Accessed on 23/05/2013).

Williams, S. (2011), '*Indian ICT Firm to Invest over $2m in Nigeria*', Business Day, 9th December, Available at: http://businessdayonline.com/NG/index.php/markets/companies-and-market/30666-indian-ict-firm-to-invest-over-2m-in-nigeria (Accessed on 09/12/2012).

MEA (2014), '*India and Nigeria Relations*', GoI, New Delhi, Available at: < http://www.mea.gov.in/Portal/ForeignRelation/Nigeria_January_2014-1.pdf > -(Accessd on 12/01/2014).

Footnotes

1. A lack of educational software that brings teaching aids such as simulations, animations and graphics to the teaching and learning of science and technology (S and T) post basic courses. It has been identified as factors that responsible for low technological breakthrough in the country (Goodie: Biz Tech Africa, 2013).

2. The network created between Indians and Africans as a result of the exchange was helping to strengthen African institutions and sustain long-term policymaking. Industry associations such as the Outsourcing Development Initiative of Nigeria (ODIN), Ghana Association of Software Companies (GASSCOM), and Kenya Computer Society were all strengthened by knowledge gained from NASSCOM, the software association

of India, and the Business Process Association of the Philippines (BPAP) (World Bank, 2013a).

3. NIIT's Individual Learning Business offerings include industry-endorsed programmes for students seeking careers in IT – GNIIT and Engineers, and Global Net Plus for IT professionals. The company has introduced "India's first cloud campus", through its new-age GNIIT programme. This offers students a higher mobility as they can access courseware using Net books to connect seamlessly to NIIT's cloud campus network (NIIT, 2013).

5

Conclusion

This chapter concludes and lists the main findings of this research work. It is a synthesis of the discussion of the concepts included in this study. The conclusion postulates that various factors are responsible for growing trade between India and Nigeria. It includes a brief summary of every chapter and tries to critically evaluate. India and Nigeria trade relations over the past years between 2000 to 2013.

This research has been divided into three sections. Firstly, it discusses the role of energy security, and growing trade between India and Nigeria. Secondly it discusses on the health segment: medical and pharmaceutical with special reference to their increasing cooperation with each other. Thirdly, it focuses the view regional power on capacity building in the education sector specifically IT and ICT sector. The overall summary of several chapters in this book is as follows:

A Focus on Energy Security: India's is world's second largest populated country. Since independence India has made tremendous progress but still it is considered as developing country. India's steady and constant progress has brought India into list of world's most potential countries. For a country like India to maintain and even to increase her development India needs to maintain her resources and to utilise her resources carefully. India is naturally endowed with resources but increasing population and increasing needs of her people compels India to depend on other countries for her resource needs specially energy resourcing (EIA, 2011).

Since long time India was dependent on Middle East countries as single source of India's energy imports. India imports 18 per cent from Saudi Arabia, 11 per cent from Iran and 34 per cent of her energy imports comes from other Middle East countries. But from energy security point of view India cannot afford to over depend on single source. This will badly hamper India's energy imports; gulf war of 1991 showed this reality and hence India needs to diversify her energy sources and African countries emerged as promising option and potential source for India in the context of energy security. India needs to focus to diversify her energy need by shifting her attention towards Africa (CII 2012: p. 19).

India is considered to be one of the world's largest energy consumers. India's domestic production in oil and gas is not sufficient enough to cater her consumption needs. Hence India is dependent on oil producing countries of the world. Oil and gas are considered as non-renewable resources and hence India must maintain cordial relationships with those countries that have lucrative reserves of oil and gas for her energy demand. In context of India and Africa maintaining good relationships as from India's point of view it is essential to maintain good relation with each other. India is one of the key players in Africa (EIA, 2011: p. 1).

African continent is endowed with oil and gas. Many African countries are world's largest oil producing countries such as Algeria, Angola, Nigeria and Sudan. Africa is also home for several OPEC countries. Over nine per cent of global oil and 12 per cent of global crude production has brought Africa in to centre stage of global energy production. Availability of oil and gas leads a nation to maintain healthy source of revenue and can utilise this revenue for their nation's development (Bhaskar: ONGC 2012: pp. 1-3).

India's foreign policy towards Africa is rooted in India's principle of world peace, support for decolonisation and mutual beneficial programmes. Impact of this can also be felt on India's energy policy towards oil rich African countries. India put stress on mutual benefits programmes and thus invests on large scale to improve Africa's infrastructural sector. India is following the policy of capacity building programmes in Africa. It is also invested in transportation sector for convenient transformation of oil and gas by constructing pipeline. India provides technical assistant by undertaking training programmes. Though India is oil deficit country but compared to African countries India is well ahead in the field of oil refining. India is building oil refineries in Africa; this is one of the India's smart move towards her policy execution on not in upwards investment India is also active in downward investment such as exploration of potential oil and gas block, acquiring legal permissions to carry out exploration and providing knowledge assistance there. Indian efforts to boost foreign relations such as India-Africa forum summit, India–Africa hydrocarbon conference, and bilateral visits of bureaucrats are proves of India's good-will towards Africa and a genuine attempt to invest in Africa which must be mutually beneficial, this is where India's approach is different as that of China. In context of India and Nigeria bilateral relations, India is persuading same policy. Nigeria is the largest supplier of energy resources to India among African countries (EIA, 2013).

In the chase of energy resources India is facing stiff competition from other countries. The main counterpart of India among other Asian countries, interested in energy resources is China. India and China both follow aggressive policy towards Africa. Both India and China are most populated countries and hence have to counter growing energy need of their population. Often comparison is carried out between India and China's approach towards Africa. Academics, scholars and researchers point out the differences between India and China's approach towards Africa. Presence of both the Asians giants in Africa is welcomed by African countries. Thus, India-China posses a threat to other leading energy consumer countries investing in Africa (*Ibid*: pp. 35-38).

The Nigerian economy is largely a petroleum-based economy. The country has now been long troubled by the political instability, corruption and poor macro-economic management and is now undergoing a substantial economic reform under the new civilian administration. The former military rulers of Nigeria failed to diversify the economy. The economy of Nigeria shows overdependence on the capital-intensive oil sector, which provides the 28 per cent of GDP, 95 per cent of foreign exchange earnings and about 65 per cent of government revenues. Owing to the poor performance of the government programmes, the major multinational oil companies have launched their own community development programmes in the country. Currently, Nigeria is a member of the OPEC and a new entity, the Niger Delta Development Commission (NDDC), has been created to help catalyse economic and social development in the country (EIA, 2013).

India offered her active supports to Nigeria's Vision 2020:20 plan. India aims to build up energy security with co-operation of Nigeria. Nigeria is aiming to increase its oil refinery capacity, to improve domestic production etc. Indian oil companies have invested in Africa. India has also improved bilateral trade and is providing line of credits to Nigeria. Overall Indian presence in Africa in general and Nigeria in particular is favoured by them.

During January 2009, India and Nigerian trade had surpassed the level of Nigeria's trade with all other countries in southern, central and west Africa. Aside from oil, Nigeria exports cashew nuts, wood, cotton, pearls, rubber and gum Arabic to India. India's exports to Nigeria comprise paper and wood products, textiles, plastics, chemicals, machinery and transport equipment, drugs and pharmaceuticals. Over time, India has widened the scope of its economic engagement with Nigeria and with the rest of Africa. (MEA, 2012b: p. 3).

Co-operation in the Health Segment—medical and Pharmaceutical: –India and Nigeria bilateral relationships are not limited only to their energy sector. India is also actively co-operating Nigeria in its health and education sector. Nigeria is highly populated country and its health indicators are not very promising. HIV/AIDS, Diarrhea, and major communication disease, maternal deaths are causes of concern for Nigeria. India's pharmaceutical investments and India's efforts of providing affordable generic drugs, equipment's, medicinal knowledge is commendable. By promoting medical tourism, sale of good quality Indian drugs etc. (WHO, 2013: pp. 74-75).

Medical tourism is one of the leading segments in health sector between India and Nigeria. Nigerian medical tourist's avails best medical facilities at New Delhi, Mumbai, Chennai and Hyderabad as well as in smaller cities also India provides scholarships to African students, students exchange programmes, fellowships plays a key role in improving Nigeria's health sector (Placid Way, 2012).

In the long run, funds raised and profits earned by hospitals and the tertiary sectors in India, such as hospitality and the travel sector that service foreign patients can be used for cross subsidising the healthcare sector to provide for those below the safety net who cannot afford to pay for their treatment. This viewpoint has been a part of the debate in the country on 'medical tourism' for the past few years but such suggestions have not been implemented as yet. Though African patients who can pay for the relatively affordable medical treatment in India can have access to highly skilled doctors and world class treatment in Indian hospitals, this alternative does not serve the vast majority of the population on the continent, primarily those who fall below the safety net. It is in this context that India's capacity building initiatives in the pharmaceutical sector, the training of African healthcare personnel in India via various initiatives of the Government of India and the establishment of Indian hospitals in collaboration with the governments or local partners in Africa need to be acknowledged (Modi, 2012: pp. 39-40).

In addition the partnership between India and Nigeria is mutually beneficial as medical and health sector in Nigeria as well as in other African countries. Nigeria avail better access to healthcare facilities by using medium of medical tourism in India and by growing presence of India healthcare facilities with Nigeria. Most AU countries are not yet on the track to achieve the health MDGs and part of the explanation can be found in the lack of financial resources available to them. In 2001, the Abuja declaration recognised this as a potential problem ten years ago highlighting the importance for governments in AU countries of giving greater weight to health in the allocation of government revenues, while at the same time urging donor countries to increase their funding levels (WHO, 2011 p. 5).

There are three major Indian companies are leading in Nigeria. They are: Ranbaxy, Cipla and Dr Reddy's. Nigeria has been helping in promoting mutual trade in good quality drugs, drugs testing and analysis, detection and prevention of supply of adulterated, fake, drugs. It will also enable education, training and capacity building of the personnel involved in this field.

Capacity Building in Education-ICT and IT: India itself is a fastest growing IT/ICT market. India's progress in IT/ICT sector has created boom in world IT market. Thus, Nigeria has much to learn and implement knowledge in IT sector from India's experience. India is helping Nigeria for capacity building, human resources, training in IT sector both, public as well as private Indian companies are— venturing in Nigerians IT sector. This will help Nigeria to increase its domestic productivity which will lead Nigeria towards economic growth. Nigeria's IT sector is lack of basic infrastructure such as non-adoption of IT/ICT in education sectors, lack of interest in implementing correct policy and programmes, lack of proper electricity supply. This entire factor hampers Nigeria's progress in IT sector. This is where India plays a key role. India is helping Nigeria to overcome such problems.

Over a longer term of past five years, the number of Nigerians going to India has gone up nearly four-fold. Of special significance in 2012 was even faster growth in Business and Student segments, showing that these ties are soaring. Medical tourism, too, grew albeit at a slower pace. In 2012, 1,200 Nigerian students going to various Indian institutes of higher learning, up nearly 60 per cent over last year. In addition, since April 1, 2012, 188 professionals from Nigeria, 12 from Benin,

25 from Cameroon and 11 from Chad attended training courses in India under our Indian Technical and Economic Co-operation (ITEC) Programme. Each of these numbers is a new record for the respective country (Modi, 2013: pp. 3-4).

India's Pan-Africa e-Network including telemedicine is further boosting bilateral cooperation among India and Nigeria. Setup of Indian hospital in Nigeria is also useful steps towards enhancement this co-operation. India's co-operation with African countries and Nigeria is not only limited to energy co-operation; India is involved in Nigeria in trade and investment and even in knowledge share, technology share. In this context, India has invested in ICT and IT sector (MEA, 2013).

India's valuable knowledge in IT telecommunication, economic, training is transferred to Nigeria as a part of India's ITEC programme and SCAAP. Moreover, this cooperation will be mutually beneficial unlike other investor in Nigeria by both small and medium enterprises. An India-Africa forum summit is emphasising importance of emerging IT sector and thus undertaking various policies and plans to enhance mutual co-operation. Indian government's "C.V. Raman Fellowships" is yet another step of Indian government to enhance new avenues for India and Nigeria partnership. Through all such efforts India and Nigeria are coming closer to each other. India's approach towards Nigeria as well as other African countries is bit different from other countries in the world. India's perception towards Africa is of a continent on which India can rely and can strengthen relationships which will ultimately lead towards better future and towards overall development.

The inconsistencies between the national policy on education, the role of technical and vocational schools need to be addressed in order to have a clear context towards implementation of technical and vocational education in Nigeria. Provisions of instructional materials, machineries as well as consumables are highly significant in the teaching and learning of technical skills. Theory and practical classes should be given more time so as to have adequate practical for the purpose of acquiring relevant knowledge and skills among the students so that they can be able to fit into industries and also compete with their counterparts globally (Idriset and *et.al* 2012: p. 33).

Challenges Ahead and Prospects for Strengthened Engagement: India and Nigeria relationship has instead been characterised by mutual friendship and understanding. Moreover, economic relations in the areas of trade, technical assistance and consultancy comprise the most important aspects of co-operation between the two countries. It is clear that the balance of trade is in favour of Nigeria due to India's increasingly large importation of Nigeria's crude oil. The volume of Indian– and investments operating in Nigeria, particularly in the areas of manufacturing, pharmaceuticals and textiles, help to mitigate the deficit that India experiences in its trade relations with Nigeria. India's booming technological economy and its increasing demand for oil combined with Nigeria's untapped oil reserves and need for technology logically imply that their relations will continue to be mutually beneficial. In other words, because of the mutual "demands and supplies" between these two countries, the prospects of future relations between Nigeria and India are unavoidably assured. Specifically, while Nigeria's future relations will be defined by its needs for India's pharmaceuticals, textiles, and energy resources (namely, oil refining and electricity), India will continue to require resources such as oil and gas from

Nigeria in order to continue to boost its technological development (Kura, 2009: p. 27).

Apart from poor infrastructure, there are deep concerns in Nigeria and internationally regarding the progress and sustainability of the country's fledgling democracy. "Misspent oil revenues mean that only limited resources can be earmarked for infrastructure, basic education and healthcare. The country's education system is failing at all levels: most parents who can afford it send their children to be educated in Ghana, South Africa, Egypt, Botswana or the West. Similarly, Nigeria's healthcare system is precarious. Disparities between rural and urban Nigerians are widening rapidly. Unemployment is high and consumer inflation is on the rise, adding to social tensions" (Vasudevan, 2010; pp.12-13).

Much more needs to be done by both India and Nigeria to ensure that they continue to be partners in progress in the framework of South-South Co-operation and further strengthen the foreign economic relations. India and Nigeria relationship has instead mutual friendship and understanding. In addition, economic relations in the areas of trade, technical assistance and consultancy comprise the most important aspects of co-operation between the two countries. New initiatives, such as India-Africa Summits between India-Africa are efforts towards establishing a healthy relationship. For India, partnership with Nigeria is of essence and strategic importance to meet her requirements of crude oil for her growing economy and energy security.

References

Bhaskar, U. (2012), '*Nigeria Gambit Signals India's Africa Strategy*', ONGC Videsh Limited, The International Petroleum Company of India Ltd, Mint: New Delhi, 5 January, Available at: <http://www.ongcvidesh.com/(X(1)S(luco3ny3xk 54cuayuv

fbfe55))/NewsContent.aspx? ID= 378&AspxAutoDetect Cookie Support=1> (Accessed on 05/01/2013).

CII (2012), '*India's Energy Engagement in Africa Challenges and Opportunity*', New Delhi.

EIA (2012), '*Nigeria Background, Country Analysis Briefs*', Available at:-http://www.eia.gov/countries/analysisbriefs/Nigeria/nigeria.pdf (Accessed on 07/12/2012).

EIA (2011), 'India Background, Country Analysis Briefs', Available at: <http://www.eia.gov/EMEU/cabs/India/pdf.pdf> (Accessed on 07/12/2012).

EIA (2013), 'China and India Account for Half of Global Energy Growth Through 2035', Available at: <http://www.eia.gov/todayinenergy/detail.cfm?id=3130#> (Accessed on 27/05/2013).

Idris, A. *et. al.* (2012), '*Implementation of Technical and Vocational Education in Post-Primary Schools in Nigeria: A Qualitative Approach*', International Journal of Humanities and Social Science Invention, Vol. 1, Issue1, December 2012, Available at : <http://www.ijhssi.org/papers/v1%281%29/Version-2/E113033.pdf> (Accessed on 27/05/2013).

Kura, S. B. (2009), 'Nigeria-India Economic, Political and Socio-Cultural Relations: Critical Relations for Continuous Mutual Co-operation,' IJAPS, Vol. 5, No. 1, January, Available at: <http://ijaps.usm.my/wpcontent/uploads/2012/06/Sulaiman_Balarabe_Kura.pdf> (Accessed on 07/12/2012).

MEA (2011), '*India's Foreign Relations*', Government of India, New Delhi, Available at: http://www.mea.gov.in/Images/pdf/India-foreign-relation-2011.pdf (Accessed on 07/12/2012).

MEA (2013), '*Pan African E-Network Project (PAENP)*', Government of India, New Delhi, Available at: <http://mea.gov.in/Portal/Fore\ignRelation/Pan_African_e_docx_ for_xp.pdf> (Accessed on 07/02/2013).

MEA (2012b), 'India Nigeria Relations', Government of India, New Delhi, Available at: <http://www.mea.gov.in/Images/pdf/Nigeria-January-2012.pdf> (Accessed on 26/02/2013).

Modi, R. (2012), '*Revamping Africa's Healthcare*', Africa Quarterly, Indian Journal of Africa Affairs, Vol. 52, No. 3, Aug-Oct., Indian Council for Cultural Relations, New Delhi.

Modi, R. (2013), '*Infinities Focus on India's Ties with Nigeria, Benin, and Cameroon and Chad*', 6th Edition 2013, Available at: <http://www.indianhcabuja.com/docs/InfiniTies2013.pdf> (Accessed on 07/02/2013).

Placid Way (2012), '*Nigerians Venture to India for Health care*', Medical Tourism, Available at: <http://www.placidway.com/article/184/Nigerians-Venture-to-India-for-Healthcare> (Accessed on 07/12/2012).

Vasudevan, P. (2010), '*The Changing Nature of Nigeria–India Relations*', Programme Paper: AFP 2010/02, Chatham House, Available at: <http://www.eisourcebook.org/cms/Dec%202012/The%20Changing%20Nature%20of%20Nigeria-India%20Relations.pdf> (Accessed on 20/02/2010).

WHO (2011), '*The Abuja Declaration: Ten Years on*', Available at: http://www.who.int/healthsystems/publications/Abuja10.pdf (Accessedon27/05/2013).

WHO (2012), '*Causes-Specific Mortality and Morbidity*', World Health Statistics, Global Health Indicator Part III, Table-2, Available at–: <http://www.who.int/healthinfo/EN_WHS2012_Part3.pdf> (Accessed on 07/12/2012).

Appendix

Organisation of Petroleum Exporting Countries (OPEC)

Nigeria is a member of OPEC, since 1971. As such they can control the supply of oil. OPEC production decisions directly affect the oil supply and thus the price of oil. Nigerian oil production levels in 2009 were below the levels and the low production levels in 2009 were therefore not constrained by OPEC agreements. In 2011, OPEC had 12 countries member. Together these 12 members owned 77.2 per cent of all proven oil reserves in the world at the end of 2009 (Hoogcarspel, 2011:48-49).

The Chart No.1 flashes some light on the OPEC's share in world crude oil reserves as below:

Table 1: Top Ten OPEC Countries Share of World Crude Oil Reserves 2011

No.	*Country Name*	*Billion Barrels*	*OPEC Share %*
1.	Venezuela	297.6	24.8
2.	Saudi Arabia	265.4	22.1
3.	Iran, I.R	154.6	12.9
4.	Iraq	141.4	11.8

(Contd.)

(Contd.Table 1)

No.	*Country Name*	*Billion Barrels*	*OPEC Share %*
5.	Kuwait	101.5	8.5
6.	United Arab Emirates	97.8	8.2
7.	Libya	48.0	4.0
8.	Nigeria	37.2	3.1
9.	Qatar	25.4	2.1
10.	Algeria	12.2	1.0
11.	Angola	10..5	0.9
12.	Ecuador	8.2	0.7

Source: OPEC (2011).

In the Table 1, according to current estimates, more than 80 per cent of the world's proven oil reserves are located in OPEC member countries, with the bulk of OPEC oil reserves in the Middle East, amounting to 66 per cent of the OPEC total. OPEC member countries have made significant additions to their oil reserves. For example, by adopting best practices in the industry, realising intensive explorations and enhancing recoveries. As a result, OPEC's proven oil reserves currently stand at 1,199.71 billion barrels (*Ibid*, 2012).

Notes

1. Australia, Brazil, Cuba, Colombia, Egypt, Gabon, Iraq, Iran, Kazakhstan, Libya, Myanmar, Mozambique, Nigeria, Sao Tome Principe, Oman, Russia, Sudan, Syria, Trinidad and Tobago, Timor-Leste, Vietnam, Venezuela and Yemen (PIB, GOI 2011).

2. Nigeria's high-quality light, sweet crude is a preferred gasoline feedstock, in 2011, United States imports of Nigerian crude have decreased in volume and as a share of total imports, with the trend continuing in 2012. According to EIA, although total crude imports into the United States are falling, imports from Nigeria has declined at a steeper rate. The main reasons

OPEC Share of World Crude Oil Reserves in 2011

Chart 1

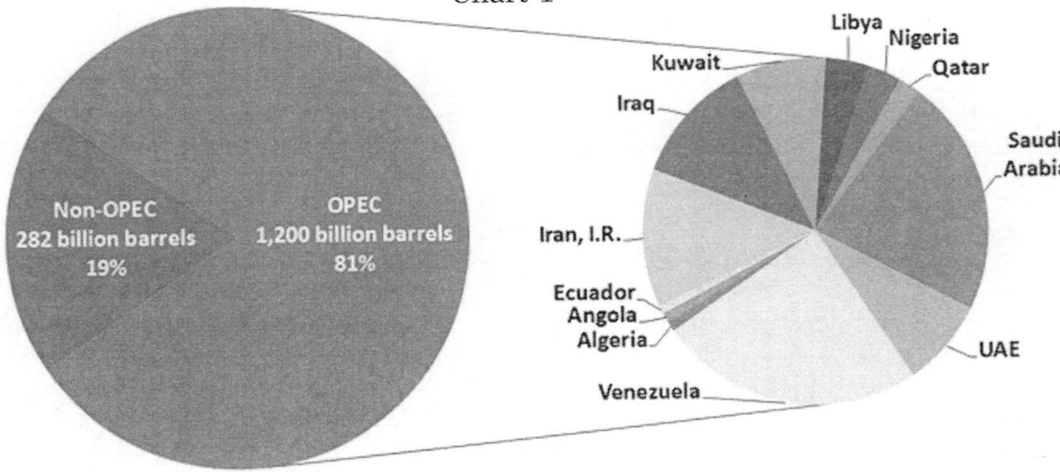

OPEC proven crude oil reserves, end 2011
(billion barrels, OPEC Share)

Source: OPEC 2011.

underlying this trend are that some Gulf Coast refiners have reduced Nigerian imports in favour of domestically-produced crude, and that two refineries in the U.S. East Coast, which were significant buyers of Nigerian crude, were idled in late 2011. As a result, Nigerian crude as a share of total United States imports has fallen to five per cent in the first half of 2012, down from 10 and 11 per cent in the first half of 2011 and 2010, respectively, according to EIA (EIA, 2012: p. 10).

3. These LOCs have catalysed export of various projects in diverse sectors such as agriculture, transportation, communication, manufacturing, energy generation and transmission and rural electrification. Increasingly, Lines of Credit are being extended for financing Indian project exports, which create in the recipient countries a greater visibility for Indian expertise and project execution capabilities with downstream linkages (Exim Bank of India, 2007: p. 8).

4. The Indigenous Cultural Competency (ICC), Country Coordinating Mechanism (CCM), Health Systems Forum, Malaria Partnership; Integrated Maternal Newborn and Child Health (IMNCH) partnership are examples. In some states, partners (including Department for International Development (DFID), Canadian International Development Agency (CIDA), the UN System, USAID and the World Bank) are working under the leadership of the State governments towards what might eventually be a Health Sector-Wide Approach (SWAP) (WHO, 2009).

5. There is also a plan to set up 500-bed hospitals in Dar es Salaam to serve patients from East and West Africa, which will require an investment of $70 m. Apollo Hospitals report that around 35,000 African patients have already travelled to India to get treatment in their hospitals. Indians offers world class medical facilities in world class hospitals and the doctors are comparable with their counterparts in western countries (Akinboade, 2012).

6. The hospital has state of the art departments and eminent surgeons/consultants from across the world. The hospital has started with an aim to deliver the most ethical and

compassionate medical care to the nationals of Nigeria (Infinities 2012: pp. 62-63).

7. Primus International Super Specialty Hospital in Nigeria has opened up following departments are: Orthopedics and joint replacement, Spine Surgery, General, Laparoscopic and Bariatric Surgery, Endourology, Reconstructive Urology and Kidney Transplant, Internal Medicine, Pediatrics, Dialysis, Radiology, and Pathology (Infinities 2012: pp. 62-63).

8. Also, with requirement of an investment of $70 m, there is a plan to set up a 500-bed hospital in Dar-Es-Salaam to serve patients from East and West Africa. Apollo Hospitals report that around 35,000 African patients have already travelled to India to get treatment in their hospitals. Several Apollo Hospitals in India were the first in the country to receive international healthcare accreditation, being approved by the prestigious US-based JCI (New African Magazine, 2012a).

9. Cipla is the one of the largest exporters of pharmaceutical products from India, exporting Australian Pharmaceutical Industries (API) and formulation products to over 170 countries. This includes the US Canada and countries in Europe, Africa, Australasia, Latin America and the Middle East (Cipla, 1935).

10. The company's shares gained 31 per cent. It is considered the fastest growing of South Africa's top 10 pharmaceutical giants and the third biggest pharmaceutical firm in the country. Cipla is currently investing $ 36 m in upgrading its plant in Durban city (New African Magazine, 2012b).

11. In 2001, Cipla, for example, won considerable goodwill when it committed to drastically dropping the price of its ARVs, from over $10,000 a year to less than $400 (New African Magazine, 2012b).

12. Generic drugs are identical or bio-equivalent to branded drugs in all respect, including safety, strength and quality as it has the same chemical composition (Sen: The Economic Times, 2012).

13. A lack of educational software that brings teaching aids such as simulations, animations and graphics to the teaching

and learning of science and technology (S and T) post basic courses. It has been identified as factors that responsible for low technological breakthrough in the country (Goodie: Biz Tech Africa, 2013).

14. The network created between Indians and Africans as a result of the exchange was helping to strengthen African institutions and sustain long-term policymaking. Industry associations such as the Outsourcing Development Initiative of Nigeria (ODIN), Ghana Association of Software Companies (GASSCOM), and Kenya Computer Society were all strengthened by knowledge gained from NASSCOM, the software association of India, and the Business Process Association of the Philippines (BPAP) (World Bank, 2013a).

15. NIIT's Individual Learning Business offerings include industry-endorsed programmes for students seeking careers in IT – GNIIT and Engineers, and Global Net Plus for IT professionals. The company has introduced "India's first cloud campus", through its new-age GNIIT programme. This offers students a higher mobility as they can access courseware using Net books to connect seamlessly to NIIT's cloud campus network (NIIT, 2013)

Bibliography

Primary Sources

African Union (2010), '*Five- Year Review of the Abuja call for Accelerated Action Towards Universal*', Access to HIV/AIDS, Tuberculosis, and Malaria Services by 2010, Progress Report (2006-2010), Special Session of the African Union Conference of Ministers of Health Geneva, Switzerland, MIN/Sp/AU/CAMH4/3.

BP Statistical Review of World Energy (2012) [Online] Available at:http://www.bp.com/assets/bp_internet/globalbp/globalbp_uk_english/reports_and_publications/statistical_energy_review_2011/STAGING/local_assets/pdf/statistical_review_of_ world_energy_full_report_2012.pdf (Accessed on 26/02/2013).

CII (2012), '*India's Energy Engagement in Africa Challenges and Opportunity*', New Delhi.

Department of Science and Technology (2011), '*CV Raman International Fellowship for African Researchers*', Government of India, New Delhi, Available at: <http://www.dst.gov.in/whats_new/whats_new12/C_V_Raman_Fellowship_AF_R-2011-2012.pdf> (Accessed on 16/02/2013).

Department of Science and Technology (2012), '*C V Raman International Fellowship for African Researchers*', Government of India, New Delhi, Available at: <http://www.dst.gov.in/whats_new/whats_new13/Result%20CVRF_2012.pdf> (Accessed on 16/02/2013).

EIA (2011), '*India Background, Country Analysis Briefs*', Available at: <http://www.eia.gov/EMEU/cabs/India/pdf.pdf> (Accessed on 07/12/2012).

EIA (2012), '*Nigeria Background, Country Analysis Briefs*', Available at: http://www.eia.gov/countries/analysisbriefs/Nigeria/nigeria.pdf (Accessed on 07/12/2012).

EIA (2013), '*China and India Account for Half of Global Energy Growth through 2035*', Available at: <http://www.eia.gov/todayinenergy/detail.cfm?id=3130#> (Accessed on 27/05/2013).

Exim Bank (2007), '*Exim Bank's Operative Lines of Credit* ', Export-Import Bank of India, Available at: <http://www.eximbankindia.com/loc.asp> (Accessed on 26/02/2013).

Exim Bank (2011), '*Eximius: Export Advantage*', Export Import Bank of India, Available at: http://www.eximbankindia.com/eamar11.pdf (Accessed on 26/02/2013).

Exim Bank (2013), '*Exim Bank's Pipeline LOCs*', Export-Import bank of India, Available at: <http://www.eximbankindia.com/locpipeline.pdf>(Accessed on 26/02/2013).

FICCI (2011), '*Background Paper on India-Africa Business Partnership Summit*', Ministry of Commerce and Industry, Ministry of External Affairs, Government of India, Knowledge Partner Exim Bank, October 12-13. HICC, Hyderabad, India, Available at: <http://www.ficci.com/events/20776/ISP/IABP-Background-paper.pdf> (Accessed on 07/12/2012).

Focus Africa (2010), *'Sector Profile-Nigeria'*, Available at: <http://fo focusafrica.gov.in/Sector_Profile_Nigeria. html> (Accessed on 10/07/2013).

High Commission of India in Nigeria (2005), *'Visa Services'*, Available at: <http://www.indianhcabuja.com/Visa-Services.htm> (Accessed on 15/05/2013).

Nigeria Factsheet (2013), *'India and Nigeria Bilateral Relations'*, Nigeria – Fact Sheet and Bilateral Cooperation, High Commission of India, in Nigeria, Available at: <http://www.indianhcabuja.com/Nigeria-Fact-Sheet.htm> (Accessed on 07/02/2013).

IAFS (2008), *'Plan of Action of the Framework for Cooperation on the India Africa Forum Summit'*, Addis Ababa, Embassy of India: First IAFS, April 8-9, New Delhi, Available at: <http://www.indianembassy.gov.et/?q=node/21> (Accessed on 26/02/2013).

IAFS (2011), *'Plan of Action of the Framework for Cooperation on the India Africa Forum Summit'*, Addis Ababa, Embassy of India: Second IAFS, 25 May, New Delhi, Available at: <http://www.indianembassy.gov.et/?q=node/21> (Accessed on 26/02/2013).

MEA (2013), *'Pan African e-Network Project'*, Government of India, New Delhi, Available at: http://mea.gov.in/portal/Fore\ignRelation/Pan_African_e_docx_for_xp.pdf (Accessed on 07/02/2013).

MEA (2007), *'India's Foreign Relations'*, Government of India, New Delhi, Available at: http://www.mea.gov.in/images/main_2007.pdf (Accessed on10/01/201).

MEA (2010), *'India's Foreign Relations'*, Government of India, New Delhi, Available at: <http://www.mea.gov.in/Images/pdf/Indias_Foreign_Relations_2010.pdf> (Accessed on 07/12/2012).

MEA (2011), *'India's Foreign Relations'*, Government of India, New Delhi, Available at: http://www.mea.gov.in/Images/pdf/India-foreign-relation-2011.pdf (Accessed on 07/12/2012).

MEA (2012-13), *'Annual Report 2012-2013'*, Policy Planning and Research Division, Government of India, New Delhi, Available at: <http://www.mea.gov.in/Uploads/PublicationDocs/21385_Annual_Report_20122013_English. pdf>(Accessedon10/07/2013).

MEA (2012a), *'Response to a Report in the Guardian Newspaper on Counterfeit Medicines in Africa'*, Government of India, New Delhi, Available at http://www.mea.gov.in/mediabriefings.htm?dtl/21019/Response+to+a+report+in+The+ Guardian+newspaper+on+counterfeit+medicines+in+Africa (Accessedon30/02/2013).

MEA (2012b), *'India and Nigeria Relations'*, Government of India, New Delhi, Available at: <http://www.mea.gov.in/Images/pdf/Nigeria-January-2012.pdf> (Accessed on 26/02/2013).

MEA (2014), *'India and Nigeria Reltions'*, GoI, New Delhi, Available at: < http://www.mea.gov.in/Portal/ForeignRelation/Nigeria_January_2014-1.pdf> (Accessed on 12/01/2014).

Nigeria Vision 20:2020 (2010), *'The First National Implementation Plans (2010-2013)'*, Vol. II: Sectoral Plans and Programmes, Available at: <http://www.npc.gov.ng/vault/files/NV2020-NIP-Volume-II-Original document_edited__versioin3_10_06_2010.pdf> (Accessed on 07/12/2012).

PAENP (2012), *'Inauguration of Pan-African e-Network Project (Phase 2)'*, Available at:<http://www.panafricanenetwork.com/> (Accessed on 12/12/2013).

PIB (2011), *'India Seek Greater Participation in Hydrocarbon Sector in Africa'*, Government of India, Available at: http://pib.nic.in/newsite/erelease.aspx?relid=78162 (Accessed on 22/03/2013).

PIB (2012), *'India-Africa Science and Technology Ministers Two Day Conference Concludes with a Joint Declaration'*, Government of India, Available at: <http://pib.nic.in/newsite/erelease.aspx?relid=080683> (Accessed on 07/2/2013).

Nigeria H.C. (2013-14), 'Visiting Nigeria' London, UK, Available at: <http://www.nigeriahc.org.uk/visarequirements>(Accessed on 15/05/2013).

The World Bank (2013a), *'Enhancing Capacity to Build ICT-Sector Skills in Africa'*, South-South Knowledge Exchange Hub, Available at: http://wbi.worldbank.org/sske/sske/cases/enhancing-ict-skills-africa (Accessed on 10/07/2013).

The World Bank (2013b), 'Nigeria Overview', Nigeria/ Data, Context, Available at: <http://data.worldbank.org/country/nigeria#cp_wdi> (Accessed on 07/12/2012).

WHO (2009), *'Nigeria Country Cooperation Strategy: at Glance'*, Available at: <http://www.who.int/countryfocus/cooperation_strategy/ccsbrief_nga_en.pdf> (Accessed on 27/05/2013).

WHO (2011), *'The Abuja Declaration: Ten Years on'*, Available at:<http://www.who.int/healthsystems/publications/Abuja10.pdf (Accessed on 27/05/201)

WHO (2012), *'Causes-Specific Mortality and Morbidity'*, World Health Statistics, Global Health Indicator, Part III, Table 2, Available at: <http://www.who.int/healthinfo/EN_WHS2012_Part3.pdf> (Accessed on 07/02/2013).

WHO (2013), '*Health Expenditure*', World Health Statistics, Table-7, Available at: <http://www.who.int/gho/publications/world_health_statistics/EN_WHS2013_Full.pdf> (Accessed on 27/05/2013).

Radwan, I, and Pellegrini, G. (2010), '*Knowledge, Productivity, and Innovation in Nigeria Creating a New Economy*', *The International Bank for Reconstruction and Development / TheWorld Bank* Washington DC, Available at: http://siteresources.worldbank.org/EDUCATION/Resources/2782001099079877269/Knowledge_productivity_innovation_Nigeria.pdf (Accessed on 23/05/2013).

Secondary Sources

Books

Cheru, F. and Obi, C. (2010), *The Rise of China and India in Africa: Challenges Opportunities and Critical Interventions,* New York: Nordic Africa Institute.

Dubey, A. (2010), *Trends in Indo-African Relations*, New Delhi: Manas Publications.

Modi, Renu (2011), '*African Health Care in India*' in *South-South Cooperation: Africa on the Centre Stage,* International Political Economy Series, New York: Palgrave Macmillan.

Sheth, V. S. (ed.) (2008), *India-Africa Relations, Emerging Policy and Development Perspective*, New Delhi: Academic Excellence.

Online Journals and Articles

Adomi, E. E. and Kpangban, E. (2010), '*Application of ICTs in Nigerian Secondary Schools*', *Library Philosophy and Practice*, ISSN 1522-0222, Available at: <http://www.webpages.uidaho.edu/~mbolin/adomi-kpangban.htm>(Accessed on 23/05/2013).

Alao, A. (2011), 'Nigeria and the BRICs: Diplomatic, Trade, Cultural and Military Relations, Occasional Paper No.101, China in Africa Project, November 2011, South African Institute of International Affairs, African perspectives, Global insights, (Accessed on 07/12/2012).

Beri, R. (2008), *'India and Africa Partnership: Opportunities and Challenges', IDSA Strategic Comments,* New Delhi, 08 April, Available at: <http://www.idsa.in/idsastrategiccomments/IndiaandAfricaPartnership_RBeri_080408> (Accessed on 07/12/2012).

Gentile, S. (2012), 'Project Management in the Information Technology Industry', *Master of Science in Management of Projects and Programs,* Rabb School of Continuing Studies Division of Graduate Professional Studies Brandeis University, Available at: http://projectmgmt.brandeis.edu/downloads/BRU_MSMPP_WP_May2012_Project_Management_Information_Technology_Industry.pdf (Accessed on 10/07/2013).

Hoogcarspel, J.A. (2011), *'Securing Natural Resources in a Changing Global Order: The Case of Indo-Nigerian Relation'*, MSc, Thesis Political Science, International Relations, Universities Van Amsterdam. pp. 40-41, Available at: <http://epa.iias.asia/files/Jan%20Arne %20Hoogcarspel%20%20Sec uring%20natural %20resources%20in%20a%20changing%20global% 20 order%20the% 20case%20of%20Indo-Nigerian%20 relations.pdf> (Accessed on 26/02/2013)

Idris, A. et. al. (2012), *'Implementation of Technical and Vocational Education in Post-Primary Schools in Nigeria: A Qualitative Approach', International Journal of Humanities and Social Science Invention,* Vol. 1, Issue1, December 2012, Available at: <http://www.ijhssi.org/papers/v1%281%29/Version-2/E113033.pdf>(Accessed on 27/05/2013).

India Africa Connect (2010), *'Indo- Nigeria Bilateral Relation'*, *Indo Asian News Service,* Available at: <http://www.indiaafricaconnect.in/index.php?param=news/2295/business-industry/107> (Accessed on 27/05/2013).

India Africa Connect (2013a), *'Indian Surgeons Help Nigerian Woman'*, *Indo Asian NewsService,* Available at:<http://www.indiaafricaconnect.in/index.php?param=news/3369/africa-in-india/118> (Accessed on 07/12/2012).

India Africa Connect (2013b), *'Nigeria More Vigilant against Fake Drugs'*, *Indo Asian News Service,* Available at: http://www.indiaafricaconnect.in/index.php? param=news/191/health-education/106 (Accessed on 04/03/2013).

Infinities (2012), *'Focus on India's Ties with Nigeria Benin, Cameroon and Chad'*, Edition, 5th Siddis: the African of India, High Commission of India, Abuja, Available at: <http://indianhcabuja.com/docs/InfiniTies_2012_Magazine.pdf>(Accessed on 27/05/2013).

Infinities (2013), 'Infinities Focus on India's Ties with Nigeria, Benin, and Cameroon and Chad', 6th Edition 2013, Available at: <http://www.indianhcabuja.com/docs/InfiniTies2013.pdf> (Accessed on 07/02/2013).

Kokutse, F. (2013), *'Indian Team in Nigeria for Tie-Ups in Electronics, IT Sectors'*, *Indo Asian News Service,* Available at: http://www.indiaafricaconnect.in/index.php?param=news/5290/india-in-africa/117 (Accessed on 23/05/2013).

Kura, S. B. (2009), *'Nigeria-India Economic, Political and Socio-Cultural Relations: Critical Relations for Continuous Mutual Co-operation,'* IJAPS, Vol. 5, No. 1, January, Available at: <http://ijaps.usm.my/wpcontent/uploads/2012/06/Sulaiman_Balarabe_Kura.pdf> (Accessed on 07/12/2012).

Modi, R. (2012), '*Revamping Africa's Healthcare*', Africa Quarterly, *Indian Journal of Africa Affairs*, Vol. 52, No. 3, Aug-Oct , Indian Council for Cultural Relations, New Delhi.

Modi, R. (2013), '*Infinities Focus on India's Ties with Nigeria, Benin, and Cameroon and Chad*', 6th Edition 2013, Available at: <http://www.indianhcabuja.com/docs/InfiniTies2013.pdf> (Accessed on 07/02/2013).

Nwabueze, A. U. and Ozioko R. E. (2011), '*Information and Communication Technology for Sustainable Development in Nigeria*', *Library Philosophy and Practice*, ISSN 1522-0222, Available at:http://www.webpages.uidaho.edu/~mbolin/nwabueze-ozioko.htm (Accessed on 23/05/2013).

Ololube and *et.al*. (2009), '*Instructional Technology in Higher Education: A Case of Selected Universities in the Niger Delta Previous*', *Asia-Pacific Forum on Science Learning and Teaching,* Vol. 10, Issue 2, Article 7, Dec. 2009, Available at: <http://www.ied.edu.hk/apfslt/v10_issue2/ololube/ololube3.htm>(Accessed on 23/03/201).

Rau, B. S. and Appaji P. V. (2012), '*Global Pharmaceutical Trade and Contribution of India*', *The Pharma Review*, 12 January-February, [Online] Available at: <http://pharmexcil.org/uploadfile/ufiles/3GlobalPharmaTradeContributionIndia01jan2012.pdf> (Accessed on 07/2/2012).

SAFPI (2013), '*Nigeria to Host Special African Health Summit in July*', *South African Foreign Policy Initiative*, Star Africa, Available at: <http://www.safpi.org/news/article/2013/nigeria-host-special-african-health-summit-july> (Accessed on 27/05/2013).

Singh, S. K. (2007), '*India and West Africa: Burgeoning Relationship*', *Africa Programme/Asia*

Programme Briefing Paper AFP/ASP BP, Chatham House, 07 January, Available at: http://www.chatham house.org/sites/default/files/public/Research/Africa/ bpindia westafrica0407.pdf (Accessed on 07/12/2012).

Sofowora, O.A. (2012), *'The Diffusion of Information and Communication Technology in Primary Schools in Nigeria: Utilization and Challenges'*, *International Journal of Cyber Society and Education,* Vol. 5, No. 1, June 2012, Available at: <http://academicjournals.org/ ojs2/index.php/IJCSE/article/viewFile/940/97>(Accessed on 23/05/2013).

The African Development Bank (2011), *'India's Economic Engagement with Africa'*, *Africa Economic Brief*, Vol. 2, Issue 6, May 11, pp.1-8, Available at: http:/ /www.afdb.org/fileadmin/uploads/afdb/Documents/ Publications/India%27s%20Economic% 20Engagement %20with%20Africa.pdf (Accessed on 11/05/2012).

Vasudevan, P. (2010), *'The Changing Nature of Nigeria–India Relations'*, *Programme Paper: AFP2010/ 02*, Chatham House: UK, Available at: <http://www. eisourcebook.org/cms/Dec%202012/The%20Changing %20Nature%20of%20Nigeria-India%20Relations.pdf> (Accessed on 20/02/2013).

Vines, *et.al* (2009), *'Thirst for African Oil Asian National Oil Companies in Nigeria and Angola'*, A Chatham House Report, Available at http://www. chathamhouse.org/sites/default/files/r0809_africanoil. pdf (Accessed20/02/2013).

Newspaper and Magazine

Akinboade, B. (2012), *'Why Nigerians are Rushing to India for'*, *NFC Media Group*, 19 January, Available at: http://www.nigeriafilms.com/news/15408/54/ (Accessed on 07/02/2013).

Bhaskar, U. (2012), *'Nigeria Gambit Signals India's Africa Strategy'*, *ONGC Videsh Limited,* The International Petroleum Company of India Ltd Mint: New Delhi, 5 January, [Online] Available at: <http://www.ongcvidesh.com/(X(1)S(luco3ny3xk54cuayuvfbfe55))/NewsContent.aspx? ID=378&AspxAutoDetectCookieSupport=1> (Accessed on 05/01/2013).

Business Day (2013), *'India's top hitech hospitals set up African centre in Port Harcourt'* Business Day Media Ltd., Magazine, Available at : http://businessdayonline.com/2013/07/indias-top-hitech-hospitals-set-up-african-centre-in-port-harcourt/ > (Accessed on 23/07/2013).

Business Line (2013), *'More Nigerians to Benefit from Indian Fellowship'*, *The Hindu Business Line* 19 December, Available at: http://www.thehindubusinessline.com/news/international/more-nigerians-to-benefit-from-indian-fellowship/article4216322.ece (Accessed on 23/05/2013).

Demmisse, E. (2013), *'The 50th Anniversary of the AU: Time to Recommit to the Promises of Abuja'*, *Huff Post*, 22 May, Available at: <http://www.huffingtonpost.com/endalkachew-demmisse/the-50th-anniversary-of-t_b_3317356.html> (Accessed on 22/05/2013).

Goodie, K. (2013), *'Lack of Educational ICT Behind Nigeria's Stunted S&T Growth'*, *BizTech Africa,* 10 May, Available at: http://www.biztechafrica.com/article/lack-educational-ict-behind-nigerias-stunted-st-gr/5993/ (Accessed on 23/05/2013).

Leadership (2012), *'Indian IT Companies to Take Advantage of Nigeria's Market'*, *Leadership Newspapers Group*, 26 November, Available at: <http://leadership.ng/nga/articles/41057/2012/11/26/indian_it_companies_take_advantage_nigerias_market.html> (Accessed on 26/01/2013).

New African Magazine (2012a), *'Pharmaceuticals: India's Generics Flow into Africa'*, *AfricanBusiness,* 19 January, Available at: <http://africanbusinessmaga zine.com/special-reports/other-reports/africa-india-a-partnership-made-in-heaven/pharmaceuticals-indias-generics-flow-into-africa> (Accessed on 07/02/2013).

New African Magazine (2012b), *'Indian Company Take Firm Grip in Africa'*, *African Business,* 19 January, Available at: <http://africanbusiness magazine.com/ special-reports/sector-reports/the-pharmaceutical-industry-in-africa/indian-company-take-firm-grip-in-africa> (Accessed on 07/02/2013).

New African Magazine (2012c), *'African Firms Up For the Fight'*, *African Business,* 19 January, Available at: <http://africanbusinessmagazine.com/special-reports/ sector-reports/the-pharmaceutical-industry-in-africa/ african-firms-up-for-the-figh> (Accessed on 07/02/2013).

New African Magazine (2012d), *'Fast Growing Belies Small Size'*, *African Business,* 19 January, Available at: http://africanbusinessmagazine.com/special-reports/ sector-reports/the-pharmaceutical-industry-in-africa/ fast-growing-belies-small-size (Accessed on 07/02/2013).

Nwachukwu, I. (2012), *'Exploring Nigeria's Demographic Potential'*, *Business Day,* 26 April, Available at: http://www.businessdayonline.com/NG/ index.php/markets/investor/36545-exploring-nigerias-demographic-potential (Accessed on 07/02/2013).

OIFC (2013), *'Information and Communication Technology (ICT) in India,'* *Overseas Indian Facilitation Center,* 28 June, Available at: <http://www.oifc.in/ Sectors/Information-and-Communication-Technology-ICT-in-India> (Accessed on 23/05/2013).

Ojeme, V. (2013), *'Primus Hospital Plans Kidney Transplant Centre in Nigeria'*, *Vanguard,* 5 March,

Available at: <http://www.vanguardngr.com/2013/03/primus-hospital-plans-kidney-transplant-centre-in-nigeria/> (Accessed on 07/02/2013).

Okwuke, E. (2012), '*ITAN Drives Foreign Direct Investment*', *Daily Independent,* 25 September, Available at: <http://www.dailyindependentnig.com/2012/09/itan-drives-foreign-direct-investment/> (Accessed on 09/02/2013).

Prohaska, A. (2012), '*China Poses Major Threat to Indian Pharma Industry Pharmexcil*', Austrian Tribune - Tribune Online Services, 20 December, Available at: <http://austriantribune.com/informationen/121091-china-poses-major-threat-indian-pharma-industry-pharmexcil> (Accessed on 07/02/2013).

Sen, A., Singh, K.(2012), '*India Eyes $40 billion Global Generic Market; Patents Held by MNCs to expire in over 3 years*', *The Economic Times,* 05 October, Available at:<http://articles.economictimes.indiatimes.com/2012-10 05/news/34279689_1_indian-generics-japanese-pharma-market-indian-companies>(Accessed on 07/02/2013).

Sonkar, M. (2011), '*Indian Doctors Remove Embedded Bullet from Nigerian Man*', *Medical Times: Aala Times Media Private Limited,* 19 July, Available at: <http://www.aalatimes.com/2011/07/19/indian-doctors-remove-embedded-bullet-from-nigerian-man/>(Accessed on 19/07/2012).

Staff, E. (2012), '*Nigeria: Trade and Economic Partnerships*', *Afribiz Media,* 14 May, Available at: <http://www.afribiz.info/content/nigeria-trade-and-economic-partnerships-2012> (Accessed on 10/07/2013).

This Day Live (2010), '*India Condemns Nigerian Bombing*', *Leaders and Company Limited,* 04 October, Available at: <http://www.thisdaylive.com/articles/india-

condemns-nigerian-bombing/77428/> (Accessed on 07/12/2012).

Tooki, A. (2012), '*20 Indian IT Companies to Hit Nigeria for Itan / Nascom Summit*', *Business World Intelligence,* IT World, 17th Monday, Available at: <http://businessworldng.com/web/articles/2439/1/20-Indian-IT-Companies-to-Hit-Nigeria-for—ItanNascom-Summit/Page1.html> (Accessed on 23/05/2013).

Williams, S. (2011), '*Indian ICT Firm to Invest over $2m in Nigeria*', *Business Day,* 09 December, Available at: http://businessdayonline.com/NG/index.php/markets/companies-and-market/30666-indian-ict-firm-to-invest-over-2m-in-nigeria (Accessed on 09/12/2012).

Zee News Limited (2009), '*India's First Successful Swap Liver Transplant*', Available at: <http://zeenews.india.com/news/health/health-news/india-s-first-successful-swap-liver-transplant_5093.html> (Accessed on 07/12/2012).

Webliography

Aptech Ltd (2011), 'Aptech Nigeria', Available at: <http://www.aptech-ng.com/aptech-nigeria.html> (Accessed on 09/06/2013).

BP Statistical Review of World Energy (2012), Available at: <http://www.bp.com/assets/bp_internet/globalbp/globalbp_uk_english/reports_and_publications/statistical_energy_review_2011/STAGING/local_assets/pdf/statistical_review_of_world_energy_ full_report_2012.pdf> (Accessed on 26/02/2013).

Cipla Caring for Life (1935), Available at: <http://www.cipla.com/Home/Partnering/Locations.aspx?mid=1295> (Accessed on 07/12/2012).

EIA (2012), Nigeria, Available at: <http://www.eia.gov/countries/cab.cfm?fips=NI>(Accessedon26/02/2013).

FICCI.Com, Available at: <http://www.ficci.com/sector/21/Project_docs/FICCI_website_content_-IT.pdf>(Accessed on 10/03/2013).

Global Post – International News (2013), '*India's Top Court Backs Generics in key Drug Patent Ruling*', Available at: <http://www.globalpost.com/dispatch/news/afp/130401/indias-top-court-backs-generics-key-drug-patent-ruling-1> (Accessed on 07/12/2012).

GoogleMap, Available at: <https://maps.google.co.in/maps?client=firefoxa&q=NIIT+center+sho wn+in+nigeria+map&ie=UTF8&ei=_CAFUsmIO8P nrAfp7 IDICA &ved=0CAgQ_AUoAg> (Accessed on 10/03/2013).

Hospital of India (2012), Available at: <http://www.hospitalsofindia.co.in/EBroucher.pdf> (Accessed on 07/02/2012).

Medical Tourism Association (2013-14), '*Medical Tourism FAQ's*', *Medical Tourism*, Available at: <http://www.medicaltourismassociation.com/en/medical tourism-faq-s.html> (Accessed on 07/02/2013).

Nigeria High Commission (2013-14), '*Visiting Nigeria*' London, UK, Available at: http://www.nigeriahc.org.uk/visa-requirements (Accessed on15/05/2013).

NIIT (2013), '*NIIT Announces the 14th I.T*', Scholarship in Nigeria to Reward Meritorious Students Seeking Global Career in IT, Available at: <http://www.niit.com/newsandevents/Lists/NIIT%20News/disform Customv3.aspx?List=a325a1cf-a064-4573-b17a-3ce89 3a0d178&ID=364#sthash.ZhCemyLv.dpbs> (Accessed on 04/07/2013).

NIIT Website, Available at: <http://www. niitnigeria.com/about.php> (Accessed on 23/05/2013).

OPEC (2011), '*OPEC Share of World Crude Oil Reserves*', Available at: http://www.opec.org/opec_web/en/data_graphs/330.htm (Accessed on 26/02/2013).

Placid Way (2012), '*Nigerians Venture to India for Healthcare*', Medical Tourism, Available at : <http://www.placidway.com/article/184/Nigerians-Venture-to-India-for-Healthcare> (Accessed on 07/12/2012).

Primus Hospital in Nigeria Profile (2011), '*Overview about Primus*', Available at : <http://aboutprimus hospital. blogspot.in/> (Accessed on 02/03/2011).

Primus International Super Speciality Hospital (2012), '*Testimonials / Achievements*', Available at: <http://primushospitalnigeria.com/achievements.htm> (Accessed on 27/05/2013).

Voice of Nigeria Website (2013), '*AkwaIbom to Partner with India on ICT*', June 29, Available at: http://www. voiceofnigeria.org/Nigeria/Akwa-Ibom-to-partner-with-India-on-ICT.html (Accessed on 23/05/2013).

Index

O